RALPH STORER is an experienced and respected hillwalker and writer who has hiked and backpacked extensively around the world. Despite being a *sassenach*, he has lived in Scotland for many years and feels a great affinity for the Highlands, where he can be seen in all weathers roaming the glens and tramping the tops. He wishes to make it clear, however, that hillwalking is only one of the many passions in his life.

D1421619

50 Best Routes on Scottish Mountains (David and Charles, 1994)
50 More Routes on Scottish Mountains (David and Charles, 1995)

combined as *100 Best Routes on Scottish Mountains*
(paperback 2nd edition: Little, Brown, 1997)

50 Best Routes on Skye and Raasay (David and Charles, 1996)
50 Classic Routes on Scottish Mountains (David and Charles, 1998)

Exploring Scottish Hill Tracks (David and Charles, 1991)
(paperback edition: Little, Brown, 1993)

Mountain Trivia Challenge
(British edition: Cordee, 1995)
(American and Canadian edition: The Mountaineers (Seattle), 1995)

The Rumpy Pumpy Quiz Book (Metro Publishing, 2003)

The Joy
of
Hillwalking

RALPH STORER

Luath Press Limited

EDINBURGH

www.luath.co.uk

Dedicated to
The Rum Doodle Mountaineering Club

First Edition 1994
New Edition 1998
Revised Edition 2004

The paper used in this book is recyclable. It is made from low
chlorine pulps produced in a low energy, low emission manner
from renewable forests.

Printed and bound by
Bookmarque Ltd., Croydon

Typeset in 10.5 point Sabon by
S. Fairgrieve, Edinburgh, 0131 658 1763

Contents

So if you cannot understand that there is something in (us) which responds to the challenge of this mountain and goes out to meet it, that the struggle is the struggle of life itself upward and forever upward, then you won't see why we go. What we get from this adventure is sheer joy. And joy is after all, the end of life. We do not live to eat and make money. We eat and make money to be able to enjoy life. That is what life means and what life is for...

GEORGE LEIGH MALLORY

Come along, come along, let us foot it out together,
Come along, come along, be it fair or stormy weather,
With the hills of home before us, and the purple o' the heather,
Let us sing in happy chorus, come along, come along.

UIST TRAMPING SONG

Preface to the new edition

THE HAPPY RECEPTION THAT greeted this book on its original publication in 1994 has given me hope that it has provided one more hillwalking-related joy for its readers. In the four years since the publication of the first edition readers have often revelled in repeating my own tales back to me and chipped in with similar experiences of their own. It seems that there is an unending pool of curious and interesting things that happen to people on hills.

A common reaction to some of the more self-revelatory passages I have written herein has been – Are you sure you want people to know this? It is a question I have difficulty understanding and answering. There are two kinds of people who write about mountains – mountaineers and hillwalkers who write, and writers who climb mountains. I place myself in the latter category, and the notion of self-censoring while writing is alien to me. Only by 'telling it like it is' can I hope to communicate what I have to say. In any case, it has been truly said that the more you find out about someone, the less you know about them. People are complex, and what you learn about me here is only part of who I am.

This brings me to another outcome of being the author of this book and others on mountain subjects: I find myself typecast as a hillwalker (even a permanently joyful hillwalker), even though hillwalking is only one of the passions in my life. In my experience, those who love the mountains are passionate people who are passionate about many things. That said, there are times, as I describe herein, when I simply have to go to the hills. As William Blake wrote:

> *Great things are done when men and mountains meet;*
> *This is not done by jostling in the street.*

In the past four years I have had many new experiences in mountain ranges that do not figure in this book, including the mountains of the beach-lovers' island of Mauritius, the spectacular Piton des Neiges on the island of Reunion, the Drakensberg of South Africa and the Appalachians of New England. Tales of these and other adventures that continue to delight and enlighten me must await a further edition of this book.

Wherever I go in the world I shall always return to the hills of Scotland, which hold so many memories. I have no doubt that many further joys await me there and elsewhere, and I trust that the same applies to you. Maybe I'll see you on the hill. While climbing in the Adirondacks I learned of the New York State state motto: Excelsior! It means: Ever upwards. Let this be our motto, in hillwalking and in life.

Ralph Storer
August 1998

Foreword

THEY SAY YOUR FIRST ascent is as unforgettable as losing your virginity, but while the latter remains forever ingrained in my memory, as I recount later, the former eludes every memory search strategy I can devise. I'm pretty sure it was in the Lake District, on which my extended family would converge from all over the country for a caravan-based week's summer holiday, during which I would seek escape from riverside picnics, lakeside rambles and similar familiar obligations in order to explore my surroundings.

Instinctively (?) I climbed, in the sense that my desire to get away translated itself into a desire to get high. I didn't have to reach a mountain top. Indeed, the idea of a summit as the goal of an ascent was a concept that had yet to impinge on my consciousness. I just wanted to reach the point where the land met the sky.

As often as not that point was a minor ridge line a few hundred feet above me. Sometimes that would disclose a further beckoning horizon, which would lure me ever further from parental supervision and result in a suitable scolding on my return. But sometimes the call was irresistible and I would surrender to its sweet temptation. Sometimes a convex slope would draw me ever onward to an horizon that seemed continually to recede, and I would have to make the first important decisions of my young life – whether to continue or give up and leave it for another day.

And sometimes I would reach a top from which the ground fell away on all sides and the clouds were almost close enough to touch and the wildness and immensity of it all made me giddy with terror. And one of those tops would have been my first hill. Nothing major, perhaps nothing even named – just some insignificant roadside lump. But nevertheless, the first hill in a hillwalking career that has now led me to write the book that you hold in your hands.

Little did I know then what a profound influence the hills would have on my my life. As a child they haunted my dreams. As a student they filled my weekends and summers. They led me from the flatlands of eastern England to a home base within striking distance of the Highlands of Scotland. As a working man they have kept me going during days when the drudgery of the 9-5 seemed almost unbearable. There are times in my life when I have lived for the hills, when the prospect of the wind in my hair atop some sky-touching sum- mit was the only thing that kept me sane.

The hills have led me all over the world. They have given me fitness, patience, self-belief and self-knowledge (the latter being two entirely different aptitudes), and an appreciation of my place in the scheme of things. They have taught me the mean- ing of perseverance and the nature of commitment. They have led me to companionship, to a group of diverse and trusted friends without whom life would be poorer. Some are men- tioned herein; others will be glad that their participation in certain events I recount remains anonymous. And, not least, the hills have given me a joy that is what this book is about.

There are times when I crave for the hills, with an ache that can be satisfied only by putting whatever I am doing on hold and making for the skyline on my own two feet. To those who have never experienced that desire, this is a most peculiar and mysterious mode of behaviour, and equally inexplicable to those who have never felt the desire to write is my need to share it with you. This book is a product of those two dis- turbing but uplifting desires, and I make no apologies for it.

I want to tell you about the hills. On hills I have experienced some of the most invigorating, scary, funny, spiritual and erotic experiences of my life. Am I real sure I want to tell you about these? No, I'm not. But yesterday I walked four miles along a lochside, kicked steps up a snow slope that led like a staircase to the sky and cramponned across an icy summit plateau that glistened in shafts of winter sunlight. I stayed in that magic land until it grew dark and came down by torch light. If the thought of such a day brings an unbeckoned gleam to your eye, then read on. We are spiritual siblings. Let me share with you the joy of hillwalking.

CHAPTER I

Why?

IT OCCURS TO ALL OF us at one time or another. Perhaps we are gasping for air on some interminable mountain slope that seems to get steeper at every step without bringing us any closer to the elusive summit. Perhaps we are trembling on some disintegrating rock ledge from where all routes onward seem to involve moves at which Spiderman would baulk. Perhaps we are huddled behind a scrap of cairn on some windswept ridge while the blizzard howls around us. Perhaps we are standing knee-deep in a morass of sodden peat that we were confident would hold our weight. It is in situations like this that it hits us: why am I doing this?

From whence comes this compulsion to climb mountains? My neighbours seem to be able to enjoy lives of quiet contentment without ever having to leave the horizontal plane. Why do I have this compulsion to get to the top of every insignificant bump on the landscape? I ponder this question not in the hope of providing an explanation for my neighbours, still less in the hope of converting them, but out of a need to explain this outlandish behaviour to myself. If I am to climb mountains I would simply like to know why. Why, no matter how breathless, bruised, battered and bedraggled I become while hillwalking, do I return with a grin on my face and a desire to go out and do it again?

The first thought that occurs to me is not why, but why not? Our close relatives the apes enjoy climbing, so why not us? Perhaps the desire to get to the top of things is an ancient animal drive that modern society has suppressed. After all, a society geared to material gain can hardly be expected to support such an unproductive pursuit (the only material gain I've made on the hill is a glove that didn't fit). Then again, perhaps the act of climbing is simply too ape-like and unsophisticated for most; it is difficult, for example, to maintain any semblance of dignity while lying spread-eagled on the ground after having tripped over a clump of heather. Ironically, the freedom to adopt such a position and have no-one give disapproving looks is one of the secret joys of hillwalking – The Great Outdoors is a giant funhouse where we can cast off adult worries and become carefree kids again. It's no accident that children love climbing.

Yet there must be more to it than a desire to have fun, or else why do I keep going when it ceases to be fun? When I'm cold and tired and out of breath, why do I keep putting one foot in front of the other and, when I've returned to the comfort of my home, why do I recall these times with a glow of satisfaction? Perhaps it has something to do with exercise and fitness – the feel-good feeling that comes from muscles that don't ache when you climb stairs, lungs that don't wheeze when you run for a bus and endorphins that buzz around your head and keep you feeling high even after you have returned to sea-level.

I have heard those whose brains have atrophied along with their legs equate hillwalking to banging your head against a brick wall, reasoning that you feel good afterwards simply because you have stopped. Such people, perhaps equating effort with pain in order to justify their own sloth, do not appear to be able to appreciate that effort can be rewarding. Moreover, there are some hillwalkers who seem to find the activity hardly any effort at all. I have a friend who is 'naturally' fit, whatever that means. He smokes, drinks and leads a generally debauched life, but stand him at the foot of a hill, let go of him and he will leave even Naismith trailing in his wake.

Bill Naismith, the 'father' of the Scottish Mountaineering Club, is a hard man to keep up with at the best of times, even though the ground hasn't seen the imprint of his boots for some time now. If you can keep to his pace of three miles per hour plus one thousand feet per half hour (metricated to five kilometres per hour plus one hundred meters per ten minutes), count yourself fit. On British hills this is normally a pace most walkers can only attain in dreams. On a good path in good conditions it is sometimes possible to dog Bill's heels, and with a frenzied burst of exertion it is even possible to overtake him on occasion, but normally he is out of ear-shot not long after leaving the car park, and over the course of a day becomes an ever diminishing speck in the distance. Yet you have only to find yourself on the hill with someone who spends most of his life in a symbiotic relationship with an armchair to realise that hillwalking does indeed keep you fit.

But why do I exert myself on the hill rather than on an athletics track or a tennis court? And why do I find myself exploring the limits of my fitness? Sometimes, after reaching the first summit, I go on to a second. In my more bewildered moments, with my eyes on the ground and my feet firmly in the clouds, I have even been known to climb two separate mountains on the same day. Now that's serious. And once I climbed the five Munros on the South Kintail Ridge and then went on to climb Sgurr na Sgine and The Saddle, all the while knowing that I still had to walk back down Glen Shiel to my starting point. Now that's almost time for the padded cell.

Perhaps it has something to do with the challenge. I am sometimes amazed by what I will attempt on the hill, but I am also amazed by what I learn about myself by doing so, and perhaps this is why I do it. On the other hand, cycling around city streets is just as risky and physically challenging, so there has to be something still more to it. Perhaps it has something to do with the environment in which hillwalking takes place – outside, away from city streets, in air that has not been breathed by others.

In Victorian times people took to the seaside to escape the dark satanic mills; now it is the countryside that beckons. They say it began in the depressed thirties, when northerners escaped to the Lake District, midlanders to North Wales and lowland Scots to the Highlands. I know the pull, having myself been job-bound in the Big Smoke and desperate to get away. Some citydwellers become so conditioned to city life that they cannot live without the noise and bustle of traffic and a regular intake of carbon monoxide; they may well prove to be a mutant species, an evolutionary dead-end divorced from the mainstream of the biosphere. If pushed I will grudgingly admit to an understanding of the excitements of city life, but I also need my Arcadian fix. I need terrain other than concrete, greenery other than lawns, an horizon more distant than the end of the street, weather I cannot shelter from and smells from which I am not insulated. Without these I wither away like a plant without light.

Surprisingly, this desire for open spaces is one thing that is universally understood, even by citydwellers. It used to be that mountains were regarded as useless because of their lack of agricultural potential: even the name *Cuillin*, those magnificent mountains of the Isle of Skye, probably means Worthless. When Boswell attempted to extol the beauty of Faochag, the sharp peak that dominates Glen Shiel, Dr Johnson (a true Sassenach if ever there was one) would only agree that it was 'a considerable protuberance.' Now, since industrialisation, all mountain country is regarded as beautiful, and hillwalkers are supposed to climb for the views. But anyone who climbs to see views in the British climate must do so more in hope than expectation, and in any case this does not explain why we perceive such views as beautiful.

Many people, therefore, feel the need to invoke mystical factors to explain hillwalking adequately to themselves. D. H. Lawrence opened his book on travels in Sardinia with the wonderful line: 'Comes over one an absolute necessity to move.' The American poet Mark Strand has a poem about moving to keep things whole, to allow the air through which we walk to rush back into the space we have just moved out of. Are Lawrence's notion of an ambulatory drive and Strand's notion of wholeness telling us something about why we walk up hills?

The spiritual hypothesis has been given wide currency by George Mallory's oft-quoted reply when asked why he wanted to climb Everest: because it is there. This pronouncement even seems to satisfy some would-be philosophers, despite the obvious counter that he couldn't climb it if it wasn't there. I know a coal tip that is also 'there' but I don't want to climb it. What Mallory apparently meant was that Everest was just out of reach, as indeed it is to most of us both geographically, physically and financially.

Mountain tops have always had a mystical fascination. In 1868 20,000 Irish people made the annual pilgrimage to the top of Brandon Mountain, where St Brendan lived for a while prior to his epic voyage of discovery to the New World. Tens of thousands of pilgrims climb Fujiyama each year. In olden times mountain tops were popular places for human sacrifice. Moses came down from one with ten commandments. For some they were the abode of demons and dragons, for others they were too close for comfort to whatever local deity ruled the roost and were best avoided. They can still be scary places today. You never know when you might bump into a bigfoot or yeti, and if you're walking in the Cairngorms be sure to keep an eye out for The Big Grey Man of Ben Macdui.

Only in comparatively recent historical times has man become fascinated with walking to the tops of hills. The first recorded mountain climb did not take place until 1492. It was not until the nineteenth century that the activity really began to take off, and only in the past few decades in western society has it become a popular pursuit. Think of all those first ascents we could have made if we had been born earlier. But would we have wanted to?

Viewed in these historical terms, hillwalking could well be the next great evolutionary step forward for *homo sapiens*, one that satisfies both animal drives and spiritual needs. We have cleared the hills of demons. We have moved in where no angels tread. From these new heights we happy band of hillwalkers can survey our planet with a new awareness and look to the future with confidence in our own potential. Take pity on those on whom you look down but do not chide them for their ignorance or they may wish to join us.

There are enough of us up here already, sitting at the summit cairn wondering what on earth we are doing here.

CHAPTER 2

Altitude

I DON'T WANT TO GET HEIGHTIST about this because there are some stretches of coastline of which I'm quite fond, but there is just no getting away from the fact that the whole notion of hillwalking involves the gaining of altitude (the reverse activity is called speleology). Let's face it, where would mountains be without height? How would we know we had climbed one if it were not for the fact that they have a highest point, known in technical terms as a summit?

For those new to the game it might help to know that one of the main aims of hillwalking is to reach this summit. It's okay if you die on the way down – it still counts. In clear weather you can tell when you have reached the summit because everywhere else is below you. In bad weather a useful verification technique is to take a step in every direction in turn, using a compass to confirm the correctness of the procedure. If on every occasion without exception kinaesthesis informs you that your forefoot is below the level of your hindfoot, then you are probably at the summit.

Advanced hillwalkers will know that this is not the whole story because of a phenomenon known as a false summit, which exhibits many of the qualities of a true summit but turns out to be a mere excrescence on the hillside, something akin to a pimple on a boil. Some false summits are nothing more than mounds rising a few feet above their surroundings. They can be detected by extending the above procedure, undertaking, using each limb alternately, several placements of forefoot in front of hindfoot (note coincidentally, this forms the main technique of hillwalking). Care must be taken, however, if you are not to become lost. A safer and more foolproof procedure involves a companion and a length of rope. Stand your companion on the suspect summit, affix yourself to him by the rope and circumambulate him at a fixed distance, checking at regular intervals to see whether he seems to have grown smaller. These and other techniques can be learned from any good hillwalking manual.

Some false summits are too large for such tactics to be employed successfully, and when they rise from their surroundings by a few hundred feet it can sometimes be difficult to distinguish a false summit from a true one. A *real* hillwalker will find the whole argument academic, caring little for nuances of height or debates about altitudinal veracity. An unfortunate number, however, seem to regard their effort as wasted unless they reach the summit of a *bona fide* mountain, and they go to great lengths to establish the validity of their target peak before attempting its ascent.

This leads into philosophical issues concerning the nature of mountainness and the difficult question that none of the physical sciences can adequately answer: what is a mountain? Straight dictionary definitions such as 'a natural upward projection of the earth's surface' are less than satisfactory. How high does the surface have to project before it counts as a mountain? How does one distinguish between two separate mountains and a single mountain with two tops?

In 1891 Sir Hugh Munro took it upon himself to resolve the problem in Scotland at least by publishing a list of which natural projections counted as *bona fide* mountains and which were only humble subsidiary tops. Choosing the arbitrary criterion of 3,000ft in the imperial system of measurement as his cut-off point, he counted 283 'separate mountains' and a further 255 'tops'. Unfortunately he omitted to leave to posterity his reason for choosing the figure 3,000 and the criteria he used to distinguish a mountain from a top. Retrospective study of 'Munro's Tables' has led some authorities to suggest rules such as: a separate mountain must be separated from all others by at least half a mile and an intervening drop of at least 500ft, but Sir Hugh's list contains exceptions to all such rules.

Since their inception the Tables have been updated from time to time to reflect new altitude figures obtained from increasingly accurate mapping techniques and to reduce 'anomalies', ie whichever mountains or tops the current editors of the Tables do not think should be in the list. Although subjective, heightist and outmoded in these supposedly more environmentally aware times, the current 277 Munros remain, for a distressingly large number of 'Munro baggers', the only mountains worth climbing in Scotland. This impoverished group of people climb mountains to tick them off a list and have more in common with trainspotters and twitchers than real hillwalkers. Munro bagging to hillwalking is like a one-night stand, recorded as a notch on a bedpost, to a meaningful relationship.

Munro bagging in Scotland and its equivalents around the world (there are even those who bag 8,000m Himalayan peaks) measure the worth of a mountain solely by its height, but there are other equally important criteria, such as shape and composition. The Munro of Carn a' Coire Boidheach in the Cairngorms, for instance, is an unremarkable excrescence on a high moorland plateau, whereas the striking form of Stac Pollaidh rises to a height of only 2,001ft above the lochan-studded moors of north-west Scotland. The disintegrating quartz slopes of Beinn Liath Mhor in Torridon are painfully wearisome, whereas the sharp gabbro of Sgurr nan Gillean on the island of Skye comes under the hand with a secure and satisfying solidity. Perhaps altitude has become the main criterion of mountain worth because it is more open to measurement, but this demonstrates a distressing paucity of imagination among the hillwalking community.

The vast number of books that list the Munros, describing the shortest routes up them and cataloguing boring tales of ticking marathons (in summer, in winter, running, hopping, blindfolded etc.), is depressing. As a hillwalker who lives in Scotland I climb many Munros and many non-Munros, and as someone who enjoys exploring new territory I view the decreasing number of new summits left to me with sadness. I find myself saving some for another day and re-climbing old friends instead. The obsession with having climbed all the Munros is not one I profess to understand, and I rue the day when I might have to join the growing list of Munroists (ie those who have climbed all of them).

So strong are my anti-bagging sentiments that in order to avoid joining these miserable ranks I have decided never to climb all the Munros. I shall climb them all but one, and so as not to miss out on any hillwalking experience, that one will be a mountain whose summit I can deliberately circumvent at sufficient distance for it not to count as an ascent yet at sufficient proximity for it to allow me every experience that the mountain has to offer. My only concern in coming out of the closet and declaring my anti-baggism in this way is that I inadvertently become the founder member of yet another cult – of penultimate Munroists. I have already chosen the Munro at whose true summit I shall never stand and I have already not climbed it, but I refrain from putting its name in print lest others follow my example and its summit become an untrodden shrine to this new cult.

To assuage your curiosity I shall tell you the name of my now superseded first choice – Carn Ban in the Monadhliath mountains, an undistinguished moorland summit that is readily avoidable on every side without missing any significant moun-

tain experience. For years I kept the name of this mountain a secret even from those who tried all sorts of ruses to prise it from me, and then in the 1981 revision of Munro's Tables it was deleted from the list owing to perceived unworthiness. Fortunately this occurred before I had climbed every other Munro. Imagine my frustration if I had suddenly, by default, found my name an unwilling addendum to the list of Munroists. My new choice will suffer no such demotion, and the good news is that I can now go and climb Carn Ban after all.

It is not that I am a reverse heightist. Of course height is important. I can perfectly understand and share a desire to climb Scafell Pike in England, Yr Wyddfa in Wales, Carrantuohill in Ireland and Ben Nevis in Scotland. This is not the same as the desire to place ticks against an arbitrary list of heights. I can even understand how the logical outcome for some just has to be the ascent of Everest, which at a height of 8,848m (29,029ft) above sea-level is the highest mountain on earth. Or is it?

I am not suggesting that there is an as yet undiscovered higher peak lurking unseen in the wilds of Asia, but merely querying why the height of a mountain is measured from the mean sea-level at Bombay. I remember how disappointed I was when as a child I saw the film of the 1953 first successful ascent of Everest. With a 20,000ft campsite in the Western Cwm all that was required was an ascent of 9,000ft; ignorant as I was of the effects of high altitude on the human body, an ascent of twice the height of Ben Nevis did not seem anything to make a great fuss about. I do not wish to belittle what I now regard as a major achievement, but today you may even have to queue to reach the summit. On one day in 1993, a record 38 people reached the summit.

Compare Everest to Irian Jaya's Puncak Jaya (formerly the Calstensz Pyramid), which soars 4,884m out of the Indian

Ocean. Or Alaska's Denali, which rises to a height of 6,194m from a 600m base – over five and a half thousand metres (well over three miles) of mountain soaring into the sky. Now there's a mountain for you. Perhaps height should be measured in ways other than from mean sea-level. After all would global warming, melting ice caps and rising sea-levels reduce the height of mountains?

As we look forward to a future of space travel and inter-galactic hillwalking, how will we measure the height of mountains on planets that have no seas? As an example of the problem, the terraced walls of the crater Theophilus on the moon rise 4,000ft (1,200m) from the surrounding plain, the depth of the crater is 14,500ft (4,400m) and the mountains in its centre rise 4,500ft (1,400m) above the crater floor. What is the absolute height of these mountains, whose high point is lower than the surrounding plain? And what of planets where the distinction between fluid and solid is less clear-cut than it is on earth, although admittedly the problem will remain academic until a new type of boot is developed for such environments?

Currently lunar and planetary altitudes are measured relative to an adopted reference sphere. This means that for mapping purposes the moon, for example, is regarded as a perfect sphere of radius 1,080 miles (1,738 km), and this is used as the base level for all height measurements, even though the actual surface varies from this by 4 km (a sizeable variation when it comes to climbing!). Thus the lunar height record is held by US astronauts John Watts Young and Charles Duke, who reached 7,830m (25,688ft) on the Des-cartes Highlands in 1972, but the mountains that rise highest above their bases are the Caucasus Mountains, which rise 20,000ft (6,000m) above the Sea of Serenity, a rise greater than any on land on earth. Even this is eclipsed by the Maxwell Mountains on Venus, which rise about 7 miles (11 km) above their reference sphere or 5 miles (8 km) above the adjoining plateau of Ishtar Terra. And the height record for our whole solar system is held by the spectacular Mons Olympus on Mars, a volcano that towers approximately 16 miles (25 km) above the surrounding plain.

One universal method of measuring altitude would be to measure the height of a mountain from the bottom of the nearest depression, be it filled with sea water or not. This would make an unnamed seamount (submarine mountain) near the Tonga Trench, between Samoa and New Zealand, almost as high as Everest, with a height of 28,500ft (8,700m) above its base. And the Argentinian peak Aconcagua (6,960m) could be considered the highest mountain on earth, with a drop of over nine miles from the summit to the bottom of the Peru-Chile Trench in the Pacific Ocean. If earth heights were measured relative to a reference sphere, as on other planets, the highest mountain on earth would be the Ecuador volcano Chimborazo, normally given a height of 6,267m (20,561ft) above sea-level, because South and Central America are further from the earth's centre than Asia, owing to irregularities in the earth's spherical shape.

I shall perhaps never stand at the summit of Everest, never mind Mons Olympus. Everest is far from where I live, it costs a vast amount of money to obtain a permit to climb it, its ascent requires a technical skill that may be beyond me even if carried by a Sherpa and it is booked up for years ahead and I hate queueing. But my desire to gain height in the world drives me to seek out hills higher than those of home and so I fantasise about which mountains of the world I shall one day climb.

All of these have non-technical routes to the top: Mont Blanc (4,807m, the highest mountain in the Alps), Elbrus (5,633m, the highest mountain in Europe), Toubkal (4,165m, the highest mountain in North Africa) and Uhuru Peak on

Kilimanjaro (5,895m, the highest point in all Africa). Also on my list are some Nepalese trekking peak such as Mera Peak (6,476m), Pik Lenin in the Pamirs (a 7,134m snow plod that is perhaps the easiest 7,000m peak in the world), Acon-cagua (6,960m, the highest peak in South America) and maybe even Chimborazo, again a comparatively straightforward climb. Perhaps then I can say, by some calculations at least, that I have stood on the highest summit on earth.

Climbing high mountains such as these, even by their easiest routes, is a qualitatively different pursuit than climbing at low altitudes. Problems such as whether you are going to make it back down to the car by tea-time tend to occupy the mind less when base camp is distant, the air is thin and the temperature is low. Temperature decreases on average by 1°C. per 150m (3°F. per 1,000ft). Even the summit of Ben Nevis (1,344m/ 4,406ft), according to data recorded when the summit observatory was open, is 8.6°C. colder than Fort William at its foot. And the summit of Everest remains a decidedly chilly spot even when the sun is out.

Cold at altitude can usually be overcome by warm clothing but lack of oxygen is less easily combatted. Most of us are adapted to a sea-level air pressure of 15 pounds per square inch, which is just enough to push the amount of oxygen we need through the lungs and into the bloodstream. At 10,000ft the air pressure is only 10 pounds per square inch and so oxygen intake is reduced by a third; to compensate you have to breathe harder. At 18,000ft there is only half as much oxygen around and on the summit of Everest there is only about a quarter. Andean and Himalayan peoples have adapted to high altitudes by having more blood in their bodies and larger red blood cells. Himalayan expeditions can carry oxygen bottles or take medications such as Diamox but the only strategy available to most of us when climbing high is to take it slowly and acclimatise. Otherwise you will suffer. If you have never been to 3,000m (10,000ft), the height at which lack of oxygen normally begins to impair performance, let me tell you what it is like.

I am in the High Sierra of California acclimatised after a two-week backpack and ready to make an attempt on Mount Whitney, at 14,496.811ft (according to the summit plaque) the highest mountain in the USA outside Alaska. It is a 22-mile return trip involving 6,136.811ft of ascent to an altitude where the body performs at only 60% of its sea level capacity. Most prospective summiteers camp halfway up but the quota of permits allowing you to do this has been filled and so I must go up and down in a single day. The ascent is technically easy. There is an excellent trail all the way to the summit and dozens of people make it up every day in summer. The only problem is the altitude.

At first things go well. From a start point of 8,360ft I climb easily in the early morning shade of pine trees to Trail Camp at 12,039ft. In Britain this would be a good day's ascent, but not until I reach Trail Camp does the huge rock wall that forms the east face of Whitney and its satellites come into view for the first time, and as I crane my neck skyward I realise that there are still over three thousand feet to go.

It is at Trail Camp that the thinning air begins to become noticeable. From here ninety-six switchbacks climb steep slopes of rock and scree to the next objective of Trail Crest at 13,777ft. Any high step or sudden movement now leaves me breathless and to prevent this I try to maintain as steady a pace as possible. I pass a grizzled, struggling backpacker who is barely moving and ask how long he has been out. 'Have the Allies invaded Europe yet?' he asks between breaths. I meet someone else who is descending because of nausea. Almost imperceptibly I begin to slow down but by measuring my steps with infinite patience I slowly but surely gain height. Until eventually there are no more switchbacks and I am at Trail Crest, where the trail reaches the skyline and there are less than one thousand feet to go up Whitney's bouldery summit slopes.

It is now that the altitude really begins to take its toll. I continue as steady as I can but my breath comes in gasps and progress becomes almost comically slow. Rest stops become increasingly frequent. I try to maintain a steady pace between rests by slowing down even more, until it seems like I am moving in slow motion, my foot taking an age to raise itself from the ground and plant itself further forward. It is as though I am winding down to a standstill caught in a freeze-frame in some high altitude mountaineering film. Soon I am spending more time resting than moving.

I sit on a boulder, take great gulps of air, stand up, move a short distance further along, sit down and take more gulps of air. It is a rhythmic, almost mesmeric activity intensified by the process of hyperventilation. Reinhold Messner says the most efficient way to gain ground at high altitude is to move quickly with very small steps between rest stops. This merely makes me feel giddy.

Yet the experience is not an unpleasant one. I know I am in no danger and the physiological effects of lack of oxygen fascinate me. In this hostile but oh-so-beautiful environment a whole host of emotions wash over me; great humility coexists with pride in my achievement in getting this far and the sheer joyfulness of still being able to function and be in control of the situation. It is not often in a lifetime that you find yourself approaching the summit of a mountain like Whitney and it is as though time has slowed down along with my pace, heightening my awareness and making each moment last an eternity. I savour every moment with relish. The 720ft ascent from Trail Crest to the summit plateau takes nearly two hours and I do not begrudge one faltering hard-won step of it.

Seven hours after setting out I stand on the roof of America. There is nothing much there – a plaque, a stone hut, a register. Nothing much really – except the view and the incredible feeling of accomplishment that comes from having climbed high into the thin cold air and knowing that in that whole wide 360° panorama of mountain and desert there is not one point higher.

CHAPTER 3

The Elements

WHEN THE WIND BLOWS from the north, rain bounces off the rocks and daylight is a grudging greying of the sky between long nights, I pull my collar tighter around me and give thanks for not having been born in more equable climes. On the equator it gets dark at the same time every day of the year, so that what we know in the north as dusk is non-existent. In some parts of the Andes it is almost perpetual springtime, with crops growing several times annually. In some deserts it hardly ever rains; in some rainforests it hardly ever stops. How boring. Thank goodness I live in a northern climate that has distinct seasons and variable weather, and how immeasurably that adds to the hillwalking experience. I want sun, rain, wind and snow – and all before I am out of the car park.

Don't get me wrong, I love the warm days and long gloamings of summer, when there seems time enough to explore the mountains forever, but the landscape seems bland in summer compared to at other times of the year. Like in autumn, for instance, when the first chill of winter is in the air, hillsides are golden and sycamore leaves turn a ravishing red and gold. Or in winter, when a veneer of snow makes even the most unprepossessing hill swagger like an Alpine giant. Or in spring, with new growth on the moor, peaks flecked with snow, hillsides glistening after a rain shower and an exhilarating freshness in the air.

Some citydwellers, whose capacity for sensation has been dulled by the impoverished urban enviroment, would probably prefer never to experience rain. The pejorative terminology of meteorology reinforces this attitude, with weather systems that bring dry weather referred to as 'highs' rather than anticyclones and those that bring unsettled weather referred to as 'lows' rather than cyclones. We even call a cyclone a depression. What a depressingly narrow-minded approach to the wonderful variety of British weather, reinforced by television forecasters who call dry weather 'good' and wet weather 'bad'. How dare they make these value judgments?

Cold seems to have the same negative connotations as rain, although any hillwalker knows it is easier to keep warm when it is cold than cool when it is hot. There is no better time to go hillwalking, for example, than a crisp winter's day, when exertion produces an equable body temperature without the discomfort of perspiration. There are those who complain about the shortness of winter days, and I would not want to belittle the problems of those for whom lack of daylight induces Seasonal Affective Syndrome, but winter does provide unique hillwalking opportunities.

When the winter sun sets in the late afternoon, as it does in the Scottish Highlands, the few hours of daylight afforded the hillwalker are like a secret window through which the timeless landscape can be fleetingly glimpsed and enjoyed. There is something fulfilling about setting out before daybreak and returning after nightfall, experiencing the transition from night to day and back to night again. When you have witnessed the complete passage of the sun across the sky in this way you feel you have lived the day to the full. And when mooolight ushers you out and in, forming moonshadows first on one side and then on the other, the day has a satisfying symmetry that lingers long in the memory.

Constant dryness and warmth and an unchanging length of day would soon pall. It is the variability of season and weather that gives British hillwalking much of its unique ambience. Not that other parts of the world do not have their meteorological moments too: afternoon thunderstorms in the French Pyrenees can have a cataclysmic intensity that refreshes parts untouched by an English shower, while in the Rockies I have sheltered in a tent while an afternoon storm passed and watched the temperature rise from 2°C. (35°F.) to 45°C. (112°F.) and off the end of my thermometer. The supremacy and fascination of British weather lies not in its extremity but in its unpredictable variety.

They say that British weather forecasts are more often right than wrong, and I recall one television forecaster covering all possibilities by announcing that there would be 'a lot of weather' the following day. But I have experienced some spectacular misforecasts in the Scottish Highlands, and this is hardly surprising given that mountains can create their own local weather patterns. Mostly I have given up on forecasts. Often I would rather not know. Some of the best days on the hill are to be had by ignoring forecasts and the expectations that they bring.

Sometimes intuition, perhaps bred from experience, takes over. On a day of freezing fog and a forecast of more I could not wait to get out of town. My companion had to be dragged to the car but I just knew in my bones that it was going to be a beautiful day and so it turned out. The sun burned away the fog and left the Highlands sparkling. We had the hills to ourselves that day – perhaps the weather forecast had not been without merit after all.

I would rather place my trust in country weather lore than computerised meteorological predictions. Red sky at night, shepherd's delight – that sort of thing. Did you know, for instance, that when the sycamores seem lighter than usual it is going to rain, because moisture in the air softens the leaves and makes them curl? Did you know that when rabbits all face the same direction with their ears twitching a thunderstorm is on the way? There is a wealth of experience embedded in such lore, but those of us who live in the city have lost touch with and become alienated from the rhythms of nature on which it is based.

For many years I was unaware of my own ignorance of such matters, my extensive hillwalking experience leading me mistakenly to believe I was closer to the land than most who live in the city.

Until one year I was fortunate enough to be able to spend most of my time on the Isle of Skye and for the first time in my life witness the changing seasons on a weekly basis. I saw the same trees flower and die, the same farmland come under the plough and be harvested, the same hillsides of heather and bracken change colour as the months passed by. I saw no individual sight I had not seen a thousand times before, but for the first time I saw the continuity.

Until that time I had not realised how unnaturally insulating city life is. Cities stop us from experiencing season and weather because city life tries to carry on regardless, summer or winter, rain or shine. In the city a rain shower is merely an awkward interruption to the normal urban flow; only in the country, where the land is directly under your feet, the sky is visible over your head and the horizon lies beyond the next block, can it be fully appreciated as it sweeps across the landscape. Rain transforms and invigorates the land. Beforehand the air is heavy, waiting for release, then the rain comes and goes and everything is renewed; the air is fresher, the land is brighter and it feels good to be alive.

When nineteenth-century Scottish emigrants left for new lives in North America and Australia, it was the rain they missed the most. When it rained in the new land they would go and stand outside their houses and remember. They remembered the short sharp spring shower, the cooling summer smirr, the autumn downpour and the good old-fashioned winter rainstorm. What more evocative sight could there be than a curtain of windblown rain sweeping horizontally across a hillside beneath scuttling black clouds? Rain is what gives the Highlands its character and I would have it no other way – a kind of cloud-shrouded peaks and foaming torrents, hillsides pleated by newborn streamlets, white breakers on the slate-grey surface of a loch, a kind painted with the subtle muted colours of an Impressionist's palette.

Then there are those magic moments that only rain makes possible: the arc of a rainbow across a hillside, a patch of meadow spotlit by a shaft of sunlight and glistening an unearthly green beneath lowering skies, a grille of clouds from which a mountain top emerges like a nunatak, a crack of thunder and a distant peak illuminated by a fork of lightning, a dying birch, bowed and broken on the hillside, rendered hauntingly colourful by an autumn shower.

Grudgingly I will admit that my attitude to rain is not always so positive. I have sheltered from rain under all manner of boulders and trees, festered in tents while swollen rivers burst their banks around me, been washed ignominiously off the hill to land in the glen in a bedraggled and steaming heap and sheltered in cold bothies while trying unsuccessfully to coax a few warming flames from a clutch of damp twigs. Good memories all. And I swear that for every one of those times there has been another when I have walked into the rain unblinking with a smile on my face, letting the rain wash away the cares of the day.

Rain reaches its apotheosis when accompanied by thunder and lightning, and if you are lucky enough to come across such phenomena in the mountains give thanks for being able to experience at first hand one of the most spectacular, exciting and enervating displays of nature. From the safety of a tent pitched high in remote mountain basins in the Alps and Pyrenees I have seen *son et lumière* shows that would blow your boots off, with pinnacled skylines backlit with brilliant and unearthly clarity and thunderclaps so loud you would think the sky was caving in.

The most exciting and dangerous thunderstorm I have experienced was in the Rockies. As I approached the summit of my 11,000ft peak I could see the storm approaching along the canyon, like a black hole in the surrounding brightness. As the sky darkened around me and the interval between lightning and thunder diminished I began to run for safety, hopping from boulder to boulder with frightening carelessness. When the storm reached me it hit with irresistible ferocity, hurling marble-like hailstones at my body and bludgeoning me with stupendous thunderclaps – CR-AAANG – that shook the sky and reverberated off the peaks. There was nowhere to shelter and I kept running, trying to turn a deaf ear and a blind eye to the forces that raged around me. It took maybe only five minutes for me to reach sheltering rocks and then the storm abated as suddenly as it had begun, as though it had never existed. As I continued my descent in bright sunlight some lines from an Emily Dickinson poem that someone had written in the summit register suddenly had new meaning for me:

> *By a flickering light*
> *We are acuter quite*
> *Than by a wick that stays*
> *There is something in the flight*
> *That clarifies thy sight*
> *And decks the rays.*

Exciting as it is to be engulfed by a thunderstorm, invisible electrical disturbances in calm weather can be literally hair raising and deceptively dangerous to the inexperienced. So it was on an early climb on the Cobbler, when our hair stood on end and we laughed in wonderment and bewilderment. Perhaps we were lucky the incident remained merely amusing.

By the time I had moved on to the Alps I was experienced enough to understand what was going on, and so when an electrical storm hit us on a 3,000m Vanoise summit we did not hang around. Unfortunately the only descent route lay down a ridge – exactly the same route that lightning would take to earth. When my ice axe started to buzz I knew we were in trouble, and when I yelled at my companion to run for it she must have detected a certain tone in my voice because I have never seen her move so fast in my life. At breakneck speed we ran down steep slopes of rock and scree as though our lives depended on it, and maybe they did.

I shall never forget that run, and even less will I forget the one time I *was* struck by lightning. Again it was in the Alps, on an easily accessible mountain top that formed the apex of four ridges and which was crowned by a large iron cross. We arrived in warm, still, cloudy weather and nothing seemed amiss until we heard the cross buzzing and noticed that our hair was jutting out at all angles. When it hit me there was no great flash, nothing bowled me over, I just felt a mild tremor go down my spine and my body shook for a while. Only later did my mind start to work on the possibilities of what might have happened. In retrospect I view the experience as an interesting and educational one, but you have to draw the line somewhere and I would be quite happy never to experience electricity quite so intimately again.

Given the choice I would rather be caught in a full-scale blizzard any day – blizzards are much more friendly and outgoing.

On one of the happiest days I have spent on the hill, four of us were struggling up the steep snow-plastered slopes of Meall nan Tarmachan when a blizzard hit us full frontal. Spindrift swirled madly around our heads and swept into every nook and cranny of our gear. Progress soon became impossible and we sat down with our hands protecting our faces and laughed at the ridiculousness of it all. Eventually we retreated. Life may be short but it is long enough to leave some summits for another day.

You do not need a blizzard to enjoy a good white-out, of course. On one of my first winter hillwalks I followed the footprints of my leaders up into a shroud of whiteness on Ben Alder's vast summit plateau, which, surrounded as it is on most sides by cliffs, is no place to get lost in cloud. It was such a calm day that in my innocence it seemed there could be no possibility of danger, and when a cooling breeze arose I was quite glad because it was hot work up there. All our leaders had to do was follow a compass bearing and remember to stop when we reached the top. But as the wind rose they became increasingly agitated, and before long we were in headlong retreat as we fought to retrace across that dangerous expanse of snowy wasteland steps that were rapidly being obliterated by drifting snow. I gained a healthy respect for white-outs after that one.

Not all cloudy conditions involve wind, rain or snow, and to be in cloud on a mountain on a still dry day can be a pleasant and ethereal experience. On sharp ridges such as Aonach Eagach, Crib Goch and the Cuillin a cloudy day can sometimes be the best time to go hillwalking. Rising air often produces cloud on one side of the ridge and clear weather on the other, and as the cloud swirls and disappears around your feet it can feel like walking on the edge of the world.

If you are especially lucky in such conditions the sun will shine and project your shadow deep into the mist, forming a disconcerting three-dimensional apparition known as a

Brocken Spectre, which cannot be seen by anyone else unless they stand right beside you. This eerie phantom seems to radiate from your body and move with your every step like a spectral *doppelganger*. Sometimes rainbow halos, known as glories, are cast around the phantom's head. Once you have seen your own glory you can only view with pity those who never climb mountains.

Of all cloud experiences, there is nothing that can beat climbing out of cloud into clear blue sky. On high mountains you routinely find yourself above low valley cloud, but there is something magical about climbing out of heavy rain into sunshine on a British peak. Once in Glen Coe on a day of temperature inversion it grew warmer as we climbed higher, and when we burst through the cloud into clear sky it was breathtaking. The high peaks of the Highlands rose from a boiling sea of cloud that lapped at their flanks. The crystal clarity of the air and the detail afforded by slanting sunlight made vast swathes of mountain country seem close enough to touch; only the limits of vision seemed to prevent us from seeing to the ends of the earth.

Only the Cuillin of Skye have given me more memorable above-cloud experiences. The Cuillin are the first mountains the westerly airflow hits after its journey across the Atlantic, and they encourage cloud phenomena like nowhere else. Skye is not called the Isle of Mist for nothing. I have had blue sky turn to mist the moment my back is turned, and seen black anvil-shaped clouds form in seconds. Sometimes the cloud descends to sea-level, such that first-time visitors can be forgiven for thinking that the Cuillin are a figment of the Scottish Tourist Board's imagination, but at such times the cloud often foams over the cols between peaks and leaves the summits cloud-free. To stand on a Cuillin col at such a time, braced against the strong wind and with cloud streaming through your legs, is a supreme experience, and if the sun is setting into that cauldron of boiling cloud you may well become a pantheist.

Wind itself is an exciting phenomenon, whether accompanied by cloud or not. Strong gusts that lift you off your feet can induce thrilling sensations of weightlessness, freezing wind that penetrates every pore of your skin offers a wonderful opportunity to test out winter clothing, while constant, strength-sapping wind is the best test of stamina yet devised. Those who live in regions of constant wind, such as on the high plains of Wyoming or the Patagonian ice-cap, are a hardy breed. There is a joke they tell in Wyoming about a visitor who asks 'Does the wind always blow this way?' Reply: 'No, sometimes it blows the other way'.

British wind is by no means the strongest in the world, but it does have its moments, especially when cold fronts creep down from the Arctic. When records were kept by the summit observatory on Ben Nevis, a daily *average* wind of more than 6omph was recorded at least once in every month of the year. Anyone who walks regularly in the Scottish Highlands will have been turned back by wind, sometimes within sight of the summit. On one occasion on Beinn Eunaich I was turned back less than 200 yards from the summit. The wind was demonic, threatening to launch me into orbit whenever I raised my head above the rock behind which I was sheltering. To reach the elusive summit cairn I even tried crawling on my stomach, clutching at clumps of grass for purchase, but the prospect of a wind-assisted flight over the Highlands finally made me retreat.

Strong winds can have their amusing moments. The bare slopes of Bynack Mor in the Cairngorms are spiked with thirty-foot pillars of rock known as the Barns of Bynack. On one windswept day I traversed these slopes with difficulty, a side wind lifting me bodily from the ground whenever I raised a foot to step forward. It was an odd but not unpleasant sensation. When I walked behind one of the rock pillars and out of the buoyancy of the wind I lost balance and fell over. Looking back, I saw my companions struggling in absurd fashion across the mountainside, leaning at a 45 degree angle and being lifted from the ground at every step. When they reached the rock pillar they too lost their balance and fell comically at my feet.

A good battle with wind or rain can enliven many a day on the hill, but extreme heat or humidity can be equally tough, even in Scotland. Surprising though it may seem to many visitors, there are actually days when Highland lochs sparkle like the Aegean and the hum of insects among the heather is almost jungle-like. There are waterslides that would not be out of place in the South Pacific, draining amphitheatres of rock that concentrate the sun's rays like a reflecting mirror. There are idyllic pools of transparent water, with underwater ledges that make perfect benches for a cooling afternoon siesta, and oasis-like grottoes hidden deep on the moors where rainbow-coloured dragonflies dance in the thermals. I have known days of searing heat and debilitating humidity, when the haze was so thick you could cut it with a knife and I gasped for breath like a drowning man while the air shimmered uncaringly around me.

But if you really want to experience heat with a furnace-like intensity, try hillwalking in desert country. Few ascents that I have attempted have required more determination than that from the bottom of the Grand Canyon to the rim, a 4,500ft climb with little water and no shade for most of the way. When the temperature reached 43°C. (110°F.) I felt like giving up and joining those local animals that practise a form of summer hibernation called estivation. You could put out your hand and touch that heat. I moved slowly, with a deliberately measured pace and a towel wrapped around my head, and the climb out of that canyon and onto the rim left me with enormous respect for those who hike regularly in such conditions.

At another time on an even hotter day in Death Valley, with the temperature at 49°C. (120°F.) and all sensible people cocooned in air-conditioned motel rooms, I attempted another hill and got nowhere at all. Not only was the ground temperature hot enough to melt the soles of your boots, but there was also a wind of at least the same temperature that seemed to get around the sides of sunglasses and burn your eyeballs.

I would not want to live in Death Valley. I would miss the cold. Even as I sit drowsily sunning myself on some summer peak, content with the world and my place in it, a part of me is looking forward to the first autumn chill and the onset of winter. Even as I dip my face into some cool mountain stream, I long for a battle in the snow, returning with ruddy cheeks from a peak well won and with breath clouding the cold night air in the beam from my torch. Are we not lucky we live in Britain?

CHAPTER 4

Terrain

IT IS NO ACCIDENT that the most spectacular area of high land on the European continent is named not after its mountains but after the meadows that skirt them. An alp is a high pasture where the shepherds take their flocks to graze in summer. When you climb an Alpine peak the chances are you will have to cross one of these fairytale fields, with its riot of colourful flowers and its patchwork of exquisitely carved chalets. Most Alpine hikers never climb above these swathes of glorious green to the monochrome wastes of rock and snow above. In fact the most popular pursuit in the Alps is not hillwalking but alpwalking, in which the objective is to reach not a mountain top but a café/hut where lunch can be enjoyed before a return saunter to the car park

How fortunate we are in Britain to be blessed with terrain whose variety puts the Alps to shame! Have pity for Swiss hikers who will never experience the joy of negotiating a maze of peat hags. Give thanks for the next tangle of heather that sends you sprawling in ungainly fashion to the ground. Rejoice in your good fortune the next time serried ranks of head-high bracken block your path. Raise a glass to the ever-steepening concave hillside, the hidden crag, the band of impenetrable trees and the totally unexpected obstacle. When it comes to all-terrain hillwalking there is just nowhere to beat the British Isles.

How much more interesting a hillwalk becomes when the best way to get from point A to point B is not necessarily a straight line. Contouring around rises and dips to avoid the gaining and losing of height is an engaging wayfaring challenge, body-swerving through peat hags is a wonderful way to improve suppleness, while plotting a route through bands of crags is an exciting and therapeutic mental exercise. At such times the mind has to focus exclusively on the task in hand, banishing all other concerns from consciousness. This is one of the reasons why, paradoxically and much to the disbelief of those who have never tried it, hillwalking is such a relaxing pastime.

Some terrain demands constant attention if it is to be negotiated with equanimity. Shattered quartzite or pitted limestone, for example, can strip boot leather with as much ease as it can shred skin, while soft peat can reduce the most phlegmatic hillwalker to a gibbering wreck. Yet I must confess to an ambivalent attitude towards the boggy black stuff, which even at its most squishy, squelchy and oozy retains an attractive primeval quality and an inviting sensuousness; don't you just want to squeeze the stuff between your fingers?

In my time I have wallowed knee-deep in Irish peat bogs and stumbled around the glutinous summit plateau of Kinder Scout in conditions reminiscent of a battlefield in a grainy World War One film. In the Fisherfield Forest near Kinlochewe I once became marooned for the best part of an afternoon in a maze of peat hags studded with tussocks of long grass and dissected by marshy streamlets – an experience from which I gained new and unexpected insights into the ecosystems of bogland. Does not the mere prospect of such a day's bogtrotting make the toes twitch in anticipation?

Sadly most of the world's hillwalkers have no opportunity to experience the joys of peat, but by way of compensation most mountainous regions have at least one alternative form of anklegrabbing terrain. The soft clay to be found in the canyons of Utah, for instance, has a sensuous quality that exceeds even that of peat; when it begins to ooze gently around your boot it is dangerously tempting to surrender to its seductive suction. In the Rockies the negotiation of deadfall (areas of gale-flattened forest) can stretch the more maledictory parts of your vocabulary to the limit. On volcanoes as far apart as Mt St Helens in North America and Kilimanjaro in Africa, the ascent of shifting ash demands extraordinary effort and willpower as every hard-won step disintegrates beneath your feet; on such mountains it can sometimes seem that you are in a race to reach the summit before it descends to reach you.

But if you really want to tackle some of the most dense, vocabulary-testing, body-entangling vegetation that nature has yet devised to impede bipedal progress, hop on a plane to the Mediterranean islands of Corsica or Sardinia. Here, guarding spectacular mountains that beg to be climbed, is to be found the most tenacious vegetation known to man: maquis.

The maquis is a region of tangled shrubs tall enough to embed small trees and thick enough to be virtually impenetrable without a machete. It is beautiful country, but the only way to penetrate it is on a man-made path; lose the path (a surprisingly easy thing to do amongst a maze of small animal tracks) and you lose your mind.

Once off-path the scorched mountainsides, the dense kaleidoscope of texture and colour, the pungent, soporific aroma that enabled Napoleon to say he could recognise Corsica blindfolded, all conspire to overwhelm the senses and induce a bemused stupor in which you are quite content to sit where you are all day and idly watch the sun traverse the sky. Rather than age you prematurely by describing my adventures in the maquis, I give you a single image of a lost and parched backpacker, out of drinking water since the previous night's enforced bivouac and crawling on hands and knees through a tangle of thorns worthy of the wood that kept Sleeping Beauty's suitors at bay. The rest is best left to your imagination.

I know of only one type of terrain more difficult to cross than maquis: water. I don't mind drinking the stuff, and will even admit to a pleasing aesthetic quality in lakes and rivers, but as an evolutionist I believe Man crawled out of the sea millions of years ago and I have no desire to return. I am a land animal. As far as I am concerned, swimming and wind surfing are evolutionary dead-ends. Whatever cosmic geomorphologist designed the pockmarked gneiss country of north-west Scotland, where there sometimes seems to be a lochan in every hollow, obviously did not intend to make hillwalking easy for the likes of me.

With the help of a map and a bit of preplanning, most lakes can be circumvented by the landlubbing hillwalker without undue difficulty, but rivers are more variable in the challenges they present and are not so easy to avoid. Rivers such as the Spey, Dee and Avon are major barriers to progress throughout most of their lengths, while others can become similarly impassable after rain or when swollen with snowmelt. Every book on mountaincraft has a section on river crossing – either unaided or with the help of a stick, rope or companion – yet it remains a skill that many hillwalkers never master, even when the obstacle barring their progress is a mere stuttering stream.

Some approach running water with a temerity worthy of Dracula; indeed there are some with whom I would feel more at ease if I could see their reflection in a mirror. They stand anxiously at the water's edge and stare wide-eyed at the barely flowing trickle as if it were some bottomless ravine. The stepping stones that will ease their way across look minute and slippery, the far bank is almost beyond the limits of vision and in between is, well, wet. When they do summon up the courage to launch themselves into midstream, they stop and balance precariously on every stepping stone as though practising for a circus act.

The secret of crossing rivers on stepping stones is to use forward momentum to keep moving and stop only when you reach a sizable resting place. It is a problem-solving exercise in which the only result of failure is a wetting, and here I speak authoritatively as someone who, despite professing an impressive technical knowledge, has yet to master the requisite practical skills. If you were to draw a map of all the Scottish rivers I have fallen into you would have a pretty fair picture of the drainage of the Highlands.

The most amusing wetting I have experienced was during a solo backpack through the High Sierra of California. The stream was almost narrow enough to jump but was bridged by a log – an inviting but greasy log, which waited until I had both feet planted upon it before upending me without ceremony. I landed in the stream in a sitting position, with my feet on one side of the log and my body on the other. I grabbed hold of the log to keep my pack out of the water, but its weight prevented me from hoisting myself up. Once my nether regions were thoroughly soaked the ridiculousness of my predicament reduced me to helpless laughter, and it was some time before I could extricate myself from the situation.

Some river crossings involve intentional immersion – it may be the only way to reach the far bank. In the Gorropu Canyon in Sardinia one springtime I boulder-hopped through a twisting defile barely ten yards wide, between cliffs that towered 1,300ft overhead and seemed to block out the sky. I removed my boots and slung them around my neck to cross an ankle-deep pool then repeated the procedure to cross a knee-deep pool. I was now in the heart of one of the deepest gorges in Europe, mysterious and silent, the river still and transparent. Another limpid pool blocked the route onwards and in I went. When the water reached my knees, with the far bank seemingly almost within reach, I retreated and removed my breeches. In I went again. At crotch deep I retreated and removed the rest of my clothes. In I went again, naked. When the water reached my armpits, and it seemed that my fingertips were almost within touching distance of the far bank, I came to my senses and retreated for the last time. Only then did I realise that I was gasping with cold and that my whole body was numb. The moral of the story: visit the Gorropu Canyon in summer.

On one even more indefensible occasion on a Scottish winter's day we attempted to cross a spating Water of Nevis to rescue a sheep that was stuck on a rock ledge on the far bank. When the water reached waist level and we ran out of boulders to cling on to (don't try this at home, kids), we retreated chilled to the bone. It was not even as if it was a warm day, and in any case the sheep seemed quite prepared to dive to a watery death if it meant avoiding our advances.

The hazards of river crossing open up the debate about the building of bridges in the wilderness. I support the American national park approach, where bridges are built only where an impassable flow blocks a useful trail. The John Muir Trail a 211-mile route through the High Sierra, has several bridges but countless more fords, some of them thigh deep but passable to an experienced wilderness hiker. On smaller-scale British mountains such fords are rarely encountered; normally there is an alternative route. Where no alternative exists you can be sure there will be someone wanting to build a bridge.

One of the main sites of bridge-building contention is the Fords of Avon, where the Lairig an Laoigh, the 31-mile Cairngorm pass between Braemar and Aviemore, crosses the River Avon. The river here is wide but rarely more than knee-deep; the only difficulty I have ever had in crossing it was when a spring snowbank made exit precarious. It has nothing on High Sierran fords. The Scottish Rights of Way Society and others would build a bridge here, but I say leave the wilderness alone. At Camasunary on Skye army engineers, against the wishes of the majority of hillwalkers, built a bridge over the Abhainn Camas Fhionnairigh in the 1960s to facilitate access to Loch Coruisk. The bridge was soon demolished by floods, as if the forces of nature were determined to have the final word.

This is not to say that there is no place for manmade alterations to the landscape. Cairns have a worthy history, waymarks can be useful (even lifesaving) and I am quite partial to friendly summit trig. pillars. As for paths, it depends. You do not have to be an ardent conservationist to realise that bulldozed vehicular tracks do not belong on mountains, but paths need not be so environmentally intrusive. A path that has been beaten out over the centuries by generations of walkers belongs in the landscape as much as any game trail or animal run, and the best of them have a beauty that actually enhances both the landscape and the hillwalking experience.

Picture a path that contours beautifully, whose surface feels soothing underfoot, that is so well drained that it remains dry even when the hillside above and below is streaming with run-off. This is a path that climbs effortlessly, surrounding every obstacle with impunity. From below it seems that there are places where there can be no way forward, but at the last minute the path takes some previously hidden route, perhaps a ramp across a rock face or an incus traverse below an impossibly narrow ridge. If the line of the route is not obvious a cairn or painted waymark indicates the way forward, but both markers and path remain unobtrusive, for the whole route is a marvel of engineering that blends inconspicuously into its natural environment.

A figment of the imagination, you say. The tourist paths up Snowdon, Skiddaw and Ben Nevis, to name but a few, are manufactured scars on the landscape. Vehicular tracks penetrate much of our highest and wildest country. Long distance footpaths such as the Pennine Way are eroded eyesores for much of their length. Yes, there are some terrible manmade blots on the landscape, but there are some beautiful paths as well. Paths such as the Victorian deerstalking paths of the Scottish Highlands, surely among some of the best ever constructed anywhere. There can be no better way of gaining height than on the superbly engineered paths up mountains such as The Saddle in Glen Shiel, Gleouraich in Knoydart and Sron Garbh in Glen Affric, where a stone staircase climbs the very crest of the rocky east ridge.

Even more fascinating are the ancient paths that cross the Grampian Mountains, routes such as the Lairig Ghru, the Lairig an Laoigh, the Minigaig and Comyn's Road. The Lairig Ghru and Lairig an Laoigh are classic cross-country routes that follow great corridors between the three great Cairngorm plateaux. The Minigaig, a 26-mile route between Blair Atholl and Kingussie, was used by troops during the 1745 Jacobite rebellion and by nineteenth-century cattle drovers to avoid the toll house on the new Drumochter Pass road (now the A9). It reaches a height of over 2,700ft on desolate moors between Glen Bruar and Glen Tromie and provides some of the bleakest and wildest hillwalking in Britain.

Comyn's Road was built in the late thirteenth century by one of the Comyns of Ruthven to link his castle at Ruthven with an inn at Blair whose ale he had become partial to. Conservationists would lie down in front of earth-moving equipment to prevent such capricious environmental sacrilege today, but the route exists, much reclaimed by the vast, timeless moors, and it makes an adventurous hillwalk. Rising to a height of 2,650ft, steeped in clan battles and cattle droves, in places so overgrown that it can be distinguished only by aerial reconnaissance, Comyn's Road is just one of many paths without which the Highlands would be a poorer place.

So you can keep your alps. Give me the timeless sweep of a land that can encompass boggy moor, clinging heather, problematical rivers and ancient pathways. Those who complain about British terrain, like those who complain about British weather, suffer from a lack of imagination.

CHAPTER 5

Snow

YOU'RE GOING TO FIND this hard to believe, but there are actually people out there, fellow human beings, who don't like snow. Somehow, perhaps because of some genetic defect, they are impervious to the wonderful white stuff. When the first flakes fall they rush indoors, turn up the heating, close their eyes and pretend they are soaking up ultra-violet radiation on some Mediterranean shore. Me, I head for the hills.

If you talk to ignorant citydwellers about snow they'll tell you about how cold it is, how dangerous it is underfoot, what a nuisance it is on the windscreen and how messy it is when it turns to slush in the streets. I listen to them with patience and pity but I gave up long ago trying to enlighten them about the possibilities of this most wonderful form of precipitation. Why should it fall to me to brighten up their dull lives?

I was once privileged to be in the company of an African acquaintance when he experienced his first snowfall; a look of wonderment and childlike joy spread across his face. It was as though straightaway, without any preconceptions, he saw the beauty of snow and its possibilities for fun. How much I wanted to tell him! About the first snows of autumn that dust the hilltops with a sheen of soft sensuous cottonwool. About the thick silent flakes of midwinter that drop to earth like a blanket. About the granular crystals of late spring that roll underfoot like ballbearings. I could have waxed lyrical about the various types, textures and even colours of snow but it would have meant as little to him as to most of the citybound inhabitants of our island.

Christina Rossetti wrote a poem that includes the lines:

In the bleak mid-winter
Frosty wind made moan,
Earth stood hard as iron,
Water like a stone;
Snow had fallen, snow on snow,
Snow on snow,
In the bleak mid-winter
Long ago.

You can divide the human race into two kinds – those who find these lines depressing and those who find them inspiriting. I'm in the latter category. I'll take some of that snow on snow any time.

One day I shall break bread with the Inuit Eskimos of Alaska and share snow experiences with them. These admirable people have no less than 107 words for different kinds of snow, words full of resonance to the English ear, words such as *annui* (falling confetti-like snow), *pukak* (sugary, avalanche-prone snow), *qali* (fluffy snow that collects on the branches of trees), *upsik* (wind-packed snow), *siqoq* (swirling snow), *kimoagruk* (snowdrift) and *siqoqtoaq* (crusty snow). The Inuit could teach us a lot.

When reports of the first *annui* of the autumn reach the cities you can distinguish the hillwalkers from the uninitiated by the look on their faces. While the average citydweller has a look of pained resignation at the thought of the rigours that lie ahead the hillwalker has a euphoric faraway look in his eye. The very thought of snow brings a little warmth to his heart. He is already dreaming of breaking trail on some enchanted white mountain with his breath clouding the air and nothing but the crunch of footsteps to break the eternal silence.

Autumn snow comes and goes with a whim and you have to be quick to catch it, but when it lies like a silver veil on golden hillsides warmed by a low sun it is worth seeking out. The snowy veneer mutes the rich autumn colours and gives the hills the look of a watercolour painting.

Winter snow comes in a variety of forms and can take a lifetime to understand. Sometimes it lies deep and soft, making progress on foot virtually impossible. There are times I have had to lie flat on such snow and move forward with swimming motions. At the other extreme winter snow can be so hard that crampons are needed just to stay upright on level ground. In between are all manner of textures, the most character-testing being soft snow with a hard crust that breaks just as you are about to take a step forward. If you want to find out about how someone handles frustration, take them hillwalking in such conditions.

Spring snow, after many freeze-thaw cycles, often has a granular, sugary texture. Trying to climb on it is like trying to climb a hill of marbles, but descent is something else. On a warm spring day there is something joyful and liberating about flinging yourself down into the cool, soft, welcoming whiteness.

My fantasy mountain is permanently snow-capped. It is shapely and pointed but has at least one walk-up route that is challenging yet within my capabilities. The summit ridge curves into the brittle blue sky and the snow is perfect, giving a few inches at every step, my footprints forming a trail that will be obliterated by the next storm. This is not a peak you can bag without effort, and my breath clouds the chill air with increasing frequency, but I savour every moment as I look out over an earth that seems newborn. Poor citydweller, living a grey life in a grey town beneath a grey sky. He will never know what it is like to climb out of the greyness into the realm of the White Kingdom, whose beauty dazzles the senses and humbles the soul.

You don't need to dream to see such peaks. They are all over Scotland in winter and sometimes in Wales and the Lake District too. Even in summer the dedicated afficianado can find snow to walk on in the Scottish Highlands. In the deepest recesses of Garbh-choire in the Cairngorms the snow has disappeared only twice in living memory. I was once part of a survey party that measured these snowbeds at their September leanest when they were still thirty feet deep. Ben Nevis and Ben Wyvis also have a reputation for late-lying snow. The MacKenzie Earls of Cromarty rented the land on which Wyvis stands from the Crown on condition that they could produce a snowball for the royal cocktail at any time of year.

If you want to experience summer snow in all its sparkling glory, however, you should go to the Alps. Permanent snow adds a dimension of timelessness to an Alpine ascent and hot summer sun allows you to wallow in it to your heart's content. If you really want to indulge yourself, spend a night at a high Alpine hut. Sunset over the Glacier Blanc from the 3,170m Refuge des Ecrins is something that will stay with me forever and the ascent of the marshmallowlike Dôme de Neige (Snow Dome), a nearby 4,000m peak that is little more than a snow plod, is one of the high points of my hillwalking life.

Alpine landscapes such as these are truly awe-inspiring and abound with wonderful snow phenomena that are sadly lacking in Britain, such as crevasses, bergschrunds, séracs and other glacial features. In Britain we have but one solitary, temporary glacier that forms most springtimes in Coire an Lochain in the Cairngorms when the winter snowpack breaks away from the corrie headwall. At the side of its Alpine colleagues it is a pitiful excuse for a glacier, but it serves as a temporary fix for those of us pining for the Alps.

Further afield snow takes on yet other magical forms, such as penitente and snow cups. Penitente are blades of ice like gothic castles that stand on the ground in incongruous and iso-lated splendour. I have seen miniature examples on Mount Teide in Tenerife, but one day I shall stand in the Atacama Desert and see the real things, rising to twenty feet and more. Snow cups are a meteorological curiosity formed when the snowpack melts into small hollows separated by thin knife-edged walls. On early summer hikes in the Rockies they can make for horrendously slow progress.

Yes, there are places more blessed than Britain when it comes to snow, but it could be worse – there are countries that see none. And living in Britain does give us one advantage over many more snow-blessed spots – our mountains are still acces-sible under snow. In the major mountain ranges of the world winter is a time to put away boots and take out skis or snow-mobiles; in Britain it is a time to break out the ice axe.

There is even one odd snow phenomenon that you are more likely to see in Britain and other places where the moun-tains are still accessible under snow – phantom steps. When I first saw these ghostly apparitions I was mystified. Normal footprints make indentations in the snow; these protruded out of the snow for some six inches, like platform soles without any uppers, their tops conforming exactly to the pattern of a Vibram sole. A line of these mysterious footprints climbed a windswept ridge for a hundred yards then diminished in height and disappeared from view, as though their maker had been swallowed up by the hillside.

Later I learned how phantom steps begin life as ordinary footprints in deep soft snow. The snow beneath the boot is compacted and becomes more resistant to weathering, remain-ing intact while wind blows away all the snow around it. Whatever the scientific explanation, phantom steps still give me a fright when they suddenly appear out of the mist.

The action of wind on snow produces not only some of the

oddest but also some of the most beautiful mountain forms on earth, from the intricate patterns of ridge and hollow on a windswept plateau to snow plumes streaming from a high ridge, from the fluted snow couloirs of Andean mountains such as Alpamayo, perhaps the most beautiful mountain in the world, to the breathtaking mushroom summits of Patagonian peaks such as Torre Egger.

Britain's most spectacular snow sculptures are the cornices that adorn the narrow ridges and plateau rims of Scotland's winter mountains. Some of these are masterpieces of the wind-carver's art.

On Beinn a' Bheithir at the entrance to Glen Coe a perfect half-mile long arc of overhanging snow forms where the ridge curves between two summits. On Mullach Fraoch-choire in Glen Shiel a delicate gossamer-like cornice sometimes hangs between two tops like a wave caught in the act of breaking, forcing walkers to traverse gingerly below the wave crest like surfers riding a tube.

There are those who say you have to be crazy to walk or climb on snow, but I have always found it a safer and much more reassuring medium than rock. With rock you have to use what holds are there, whereas with snow you can make your own. I exaggerate, and I am not suggesting you head for the nearest ice-fall with a pick and shovel, but there is something creative and satisfying about carving your way with an ice axe up a virgin snow slope.

Snow can also be more fun than rock especially when you can slide down it using your ice axe as a brake, technically known as glissading to make it seem more skillful. It has been said that there are three types of glissade – standing, sitting and uncontrolled, and that they usually follow each other in quick succession. For this reason Safetyman usually advises against glissading, but Safetyman always was a killjoy. I here and now admit to loving glissading. If I have any concern it is not for my body but for the seat of my expensive overtrousers. This is where an item of equipment known as a polybag, available from all good mountaineering shops, comes in useful, but far be it for me to recommend the use of such – consult an instruction manual.

Cornices can also be great fun, providing you treat them with due deference (unlike an acquaintance of mine who liked to tunnel into them to brew up sheltered from the storm). Many times in the depths of winter I stop on descent to play around on the overhanging snowbanks of a frozen stream. I usually end up on my back with a collapsed cornice on my chest. but I never said I was any good at this sort of thing.

Similar manoeuvres on the hill are best tackled with the aid of a rope. In Raeburn's Gully in Coire Ardair I took off my mitts to photograph my partner leading over a cornice and by the time my turn came to follow I had the hot-aches. In excruciating pain I attacked the cornice using a technique I can only describe as reckless flailing. The cornice soon succumbed to my bombardment and duly collapsed around me. My partner's face bore an expression of pure glee as he hauled me ignominiously over the lip.

Normally this kind of snow climbing is well out of my league. My numerous failed attempts at it have become legendary in certain mountaineering club circles. Another time, for instance, we retreated from South Castle Gully on Ben Nevis, a gully sometimes used by climbers as a winter descent route but one which proved too much for us on this particular December day. This time the laugh was on my partner as he took the first abseil down from our high point. With one great leap he took to the air like a trapeze artist. On re-entry I saw his legs brace to take the impact with the snow, then he hit the snow and with a great whoop of surprise disappeared from sight. He had abseiled into a snow cave. I was grinning from ear to ear as I hauled him out.

Another time, festooned with ice hammers and screws, he led an ice pitch well beyond my meagre capabilities; how he expected me to follow I'll never know, but fortunately he became stuck so I was spared the embarrassment. Unfortunately for him he couldn't reverse the icefall and could find no anchor for an abseil. I didn't see the problem – all he had to do was jump. He was only about twenty feet above me and I had a good belay on a snowy ledge that was wide enough to allow him at least a couple of rolls after landing before he went over the edge. He took so long thinking about it that I began to get very cold and eventually I almost had to pull him down. Some people have no concern for others.

Despite our escapades, or perhaps because of them, for who else could understand the shared joy and shared dependency of such moments, we remained good friends. I have two so-called friends, however, whom, because of snow, I can never forgive. We were to meet beside Loch Laggan on Friday evening for a weekend of camping and walking. My friends set out in the early afternoon, just before a blizzard struck the Highlands, and by the time my partner and I were able to leave in the early evening blocked roads prevented us from joining them.

That blizzard produced one of the heaviest snowfalls ever recorded in the Highlands and I missed out on it. Roads and railways were blocked for a week. Wasn't I lucky, said my colleagues at work on Monday morning, wasn't I lucky to have avoided the worst of it. It was almost as if their concern was calculated to frustrate me even more.

Two weeks later, as I sat and listened to my erstwhile friends describe their experiences, my envy knew no bounds. On the Friday night they had erected their tent in heavy snow on

Lagganside. The following morning they awoke to a winter wonderland and spent the day playing in it. By the following morning again the snow was drifting and they were in danger of being buried. Surely they could have shovelled it aside, I suggested (and still suggest) to them. Surely they could have built some kind of wall of hardpacked snow to shelter from the wind. Or an igloo. No, they said, they had to abandon tent. This lack of fortitude on their part is my only crumb of comfort in the whole sorry episode.

They spent the day struggling through drifts to reach the nearest habitation, which just happened to be a hotel, and there they spent the next five days playing in the snow until the roads were opened. As I say, and I am normally not someone to bear a grudge, there are some things that should not be forgiven.

But let me not end on a sour note. Here are some images, chosen almost at random, which illustrate for me the joy of snow.

The trail out of the car park cuts between high banks that are so heavy with windblown snow that cornices on each side are meeting in the middle, forming a tunnel. Christine walks into the tunnel like into an icy inferno, the snow swirling wildly at her back and closing like curtains behind her.

Paul and I gasp as we tackle a second Munro on a Glen Coe ridge. The snow has been soft, the weather heavy, the going strength sapping. There is nothing to see in the monochrome landscape and nothing to do but to follow the ridge upwards. Suddenly he stops, turns to me and says, 'You know, I can't understand anyone who doesn't like hillwalking.'

Ian strides along a Glen Affric ridge. His body and rucksack are encrusted in snow. I can hardly make him out in the thick cloud and swirling spindrift. When he turns I catch up with him and see a broad grin framed by an icicle-encrusted beard.

Without a word he turns on his heels and strides out again. I have an image of him in mid-stride, heading cheerfully into the unknown, a speckled white figure, his foot raised for the next stride, his Vibram sole glistening white.

At the south summit of Buachaille Etive Beag the route onwards drops abruptly out of sight into a whirlpool of cloud. I sit in the snow and struggle with numbed hands to fix crampons to my boots while the blizzard rocks me on my haunches and blasts my face with hail like nails. By warming my hands intermittently on my crotch I succeed in fastening my crampon straps, and after what seems an interminable amount of time I am ready to move again. I take a deep breath and crawl to the edge. The blizzard abates, the cloud clears and I see I am standing at the lip of an abrupt drop of all of five feet. Twenty seconds later I am taking my crampons off again and laughing. A sparkling snow ridge beckons onwards to the main summit.

Robin stands alone on the sharpest section of the Tarmachan Ridge. While the rest of us eat lunch this most gregarious of people has wandered off alone to commune with nature in a way that he will later deny with embarrassment. He stands there looking away from us, hands thrust deep into duvet pockets, gazing wistfully at an ocean of white, mountain upon mountain for the climbing.

CHAPTER 6

Nocturne

IF I'VE HEARD IT ONCE I've heard it a thousand times: 'The view must be wonderful.' Searching for some reason to climb mountains with which they can identify, flatlanders latch on to the only notion that makes sense to their gravity-bound minds – hillwalkers climb mountains to see the view. I like to confound them. 'The view? What view? It was cloudy when we set out and it was cloudy when we got back.' They look at me as though I inhabit a mysterious world where cause and effect no longer apply. Even more perplexing to them, I climb mountains in the dark.

The urge does not come over me that often, but when it does it has to be satisfied. The catalyst might be a wisp of cloud bisecting a full moon or the vague outline of a mountain briefly glimpsed across the moor at twilight. Once it was the spectacle of Orion rising over Glen Coe as the moon flooded the Blackmount with ambient silver light. Another time it was conical Stroud Peak in the Rockies, its north face like a black hole as the moon backlit its shimmering outline. Sometimes it only takes a cool evening breeze or the clearing cloud and freshening air that follows a rainstorm to get me heading for the setting sun.

Nightwalking is a mesmeric activity unlike anything that can be experienced during the day. With no distant views to distract the eye, the universe contracts to the few square yards of earth over which you are moving. On a moonless, starless night nothing exists outside the circle circumscribed by the beam from your torch. You are the centre and sole inhabitant of a universe that moves at your command through black space. Time becomes a meaningless dimension because no summit or end-point to the walk can be seen. The act of placing one foot in front of the other is sufficient unto itself. You become rooted to the place and the moment, a solitary particle in the space-time continuum.

Not only is there less light but there is also less sound. A distant road has less traffic, there are no birds, any animals still about move more stealthily. In the still of the night the sound of movement – the whoosh of a bat returning to its cave, the rumble of a falling rock loosened from a cliff by night frost – can spin you around on your heels. Sometimes, especially when alone, your heart may skip a beat.

Detailed routefinding becomes impossible. You can plan your grand strategy for the ascent but local tactics for avoidance of crags, bogs and other obstacles cannot be employed when the hillside reveals itself only in tantalisingly small torchlit segments. Everything is contingent. It is the existential approach to hill-walking.

You still climb to reach the summit, but it is not dangled before you like a carrot to ease the ascent. The ascent is the thing; it becomes enjoyable in its own right, not as a means to an end. When the summit eventually comes under your torch beam it is a surprise. When you finally stand beside the cairn there is no need for a grand view or a feeling of relief that the ascent is over. Nightwalking tunes you in to yourself in such a way that you will have achieved a peaceful equilibrium long before you reach the summit. The summit is an anticlimax. It merely marks the point at which you turn around.

'Don't do it!' cries Safetyman. Are you not more likely to twist an ankle or fall into a stream or slip on an unseen patch of ice at night? Yes, you are. Will you not be in more trouble if the cloud descends? Yes, you will. Are you not more likely to get lost at night? Yes, you are. Will you not have problems if your torch fails? Yes, you will. There are risks in all hillwalking pursuits. The competent hillwalker is not the one who avoids all risk by staying at home and reading about it instead, but the one who is able to assess the risks and who has the mountaincraft to deal with them. A useful precaution, for example, is to carry a chemical lightstick that will give you enough light to get off the hill in case of torch failure.

I often hear from those who haven't tried it that nightwalking, like caving, must be a claustrophobic and oppressive activity, because you are surrounded by blackness. On the contrary, darkness gives a sensation of limitless space. Wherever the torch beam penetrates it never reaches a horizon; there is always something further, out of reach, an infinite universe of possibility. Nightwalking is less likely to induce claustrophobia than a feeling of freefalling through space. Sometimes this is unnerving, other times amusing.

We were descending from the Crianlarich Hills when, owing to a miscalculation, we were overtaken by darkness. For once we had no torches and felt suitably foolish as we completed the descent beside a waterfall in the time-honoured seated position. The path was good and we could see cars on the road less than half a mile away, but a simple absence of light reduced our rate of progress to that of a soporific snail. The ridiculousness of probing down into the darkness and feeling with an outstretched toe for the next footstep reduced us to fits of giggling.

Once we had negotiated the waterfall we aimed for a light emanating from what turned out to be a farmhouse and were soon feeling doubly foolish. Our nocturnal ramblings through the farmyard aroused the curiosity of the farmer, who gave us a fright by suddenly appearing from behind a dry-stone wall. We explained to him that our intentions were completely honourable. Didn't we have torches, he wanted to know? Of course we did, I lied impeccably, but we were saving them for when we really needed them. He stared at us with a puzzled look on his face, as though we must be on some high-carrot diet, and he was lost for words when we bade him farewell and continued on our way with as much nonchalance as we could muster, trying to walk normally without tripping over anything.

Another time, everything was planned. We had climbed the three tops of Beinn a' Ghlo on a short winter's day and when night fell we simply donned head torches and continued on our way. Our return route involved a long traverse across a steep, snowbound hillside corrugated by wind into a vertical frozen, swollen sea. But we couldn't see it. So uniform was the surface of the snow that a torch beam could pick out no irregularity in it nor any indication of angle, including whether the next step was uphill or downhill.

If you have never walked across terrain where between one step and the next the unseen surface may vary through a vertical range of several feet, it is a difficult sensation to imagine. We attacked the waves of snow blindly, clambering over some, breaking through others with sheer brute force. We staggered around like rejects from a remake of 'Pinocchio', with arms flailing uselessly in an effort to maintain balance. It would have been funny except that the constantly shifting angle of the ground and the lack of a visible horizon induced feelings of nausea. It is the only time on a mountain when I have felt seasick.

More commonly, nightwalking induces feelings of wonder. There are few things more romantic than a moonlit winter ascent, when the ethereal silence is broken only by the crunch of snow beneath your feet, and your moonshadow gyrates faithfully beside you at every step. On such occasions the world has a strange and intoxicating beauty. So it was when I walked from

Derry Lodge to Linn of Dee, my companion and I unconsciously drifting a hundred yards apart to allow us our own space in that great silver-grey landscape. At the end of the walk we exchanged a glance and the euphoria on our faces made words superfluous.

To some a romantic evening means a warm fire, low lights and soft music, but what could be more romantic than being out in the wilds at night with a loved one, serenaded by the music of the night, your way illuminated by a canopy of sparkling stars, your bodies warmed by exertion and elation? Returning to the roadside from Beinn Dhearg Mhor, a chill wind hurried us along a path so wide that we could walk hand in hand, buoyed by gusts of wind. At a wooden bridge we paused for a bite to eat and lay down to reduce wind resistance, huddling together beneath wildly flailing branches.

In Glen Affric there was not a breath of wind nor a star to be seen in the overcast sky. Every word we spoke in that hushed, vaulted atmosphere had such resonant clarity that we revelled in the sound of each other's voice. Through air so still it was a shame to disturb it by breathing, we strolled by torch-light along the beautiful swathe of path above Loch Affric, succumbing to the silence and shared peacefulness.

When it comes to romantic moments there are few more special than the onset of night itself, given appropriate atmospheric conditions for sunset viewing. For me dawns have never been as spectacular, although I know of no meteorological reason why this should be so (and admittedly I have seen less of them). In movies they sometimes shoot dawn through coloured filters and run it backwards to create the effect of a dramatic sunset, but I have never seen anything on film that remotely approaches the spectacle of a true mountain sunset.

Picture a lake at 11,000ft in the Sierra Nevada of California, its ice-floed surface broken at regular intervals into pools of still water. Across the lake rise impossibly perfect peaks streaked with snow behind which the fireball sun slowly sinks. As it sinks the sky streaks yellow, the snow on the mountain behind me burns red and the pools of water reflect each minute change in the kaleidoscopic spectacle like a shifting patchwork quilt.

Imagine a twenty-mile skyline of Rocky Mountain summits hanging like a frieze on the horizon. The setting sun hits them full, turning them not red but, tonight, a ghostly almost transparent white. Swiftly moving clouds combine with the sinking sun to create an ever-changing pattern of light and shade, highlighting first one peak then another. Eventually only the highest peak remains in light, king of the range, and then that too is gathered by the darkness. And throughout there is not one jot of colour anywhere – a magnificent monochrome sunset.

One of the most astonishing natural spectacles I have seen occurred on the east side of the Sierra at Mono Lake, which is famous for its pinnacles of coral-like tufa that rise from the lake's surface. As darkness fell, with black clouds over the Sierra and barely a spark of light in the sky, we were ready to leave when the sky opened up like a Pandora's box and gold and red fingers of light reached out from over the Sierra, like a diabolical hand grasping for the now silhouetted towers of tufa. Never have I seen a more terrifyingly beautiful sight.

Sierra Nevada and Rocky Mountain sunset watchers are lucky, because these mountain ranges run along a north-south axis and many of their peaks catch the full glory of the setting sun. British and European sunset seekers have to be more cunning; it can take some years to discover the best viewpoints and the best time of year and night to go there. The best viewing conditions are often found not in the valleys but on the tops, and there is no better perch from which to view the advancing darkness than the Cuillin Ridge on the Isle of Skye.

It used to be that we would plan our summer days on the Cuillin to arrive on our last peak no later than 10.30pm, ready for the start of the light show. Sometimes our expectations were so high that we would take up our positions early and wait for two hours or more. I say 'used to' because it does seem to me that Highland sunsets are not what they once were. Perhaps these 'good old days' exist only in fond memory, but I do worry about the ozone layer, acid rain and such matters.

The summer sun sets over The Sea of the Hebrides between 10.30pm and 10.45pm. If the sky is clear the burning orb of the sun is extinguished by the water in a matter of seconds, leaving behind a rich magenta glow as testament to its passage. I have photographs of companions silhouetted against such skies, an image of man and the cosmos that transcends the mere pictorial and gives some inkling of the humbling power of nature. If there is patchy cloud cover the dying light is diffused into more spectacular effects; I swear I have seen all-colours of the rainbow in such skies.

Even after the sun has gone not one of us moves when there is cloud in the sky, because we know the best is yet to come. As the sun continues to sink, out of sight now below the horizon, its light strikes the clouds above our heads, girdling the landscape with a glorious new halo of colour. The clouds turn from black to pink to red and then to black again before the sun finally lets go of its hold on this part of the planet. Only then, without a word, for we have done this often, do we pack our rucksacks and head for the glen. There is a 3,000ft descent ahead of us but we know the best scree runs down from the best viewpoints and we descend quickly with a skill gained from many nights of practice.

Sunset is not the only spectacle vouchsafed to night-walkers. Stars are a revelation when seen from a countryside devoid of ambient light; it is no accident that astronomers like to build their observatories on mountain tops. The depth and density of the Milky Way when viewed in clear mountain air is spellbinding and can only make one wonder what extra-terrestrial mountains await future generations of spacewalkers.

Those of us who live well into the northern hemisphere are also fortunate in being able to see one of the other great displays of the night sky – the Aurora Borealis. It is a shy phenomenon at British latitudes but will eventually show itself to all patient creatures of the night. Some displays are better than others, but I have seen a couple that have rooted me to the spot. One was in Glen Affric after a heavy February snowfall. Vast curtains of white light billowed over the hills in shifting patterns, sometimes coming so close that it seemed you could reach out and touch them. In Finland they call this phenomenon *revontuulet* (fox-tail light), because they say it is caused by a giant fox-tail waving across the sky. The other display I witnessed occurred in the Lairig Ghru one frosty October night. Soft rippling light spread out across the sky, making the outlines of the mountains shimmer. I watched mesmerised and shivering, unable to seek the warmth of my tent until the display ended.

And then the deep enveloping darkness.

CHAPTER 7

Camping

WOULD YOU BELIEVE THERE are hillwalkers who have never slept under canvas? Apparently their love affair with the hills goes no deeper than a one-day stand. They say they like their creature comforts too much to camp – a bath to wash the hill from their bodies, a hot meal to replenish lost energy, a mattress on which to rest weary limbs. But what makes them think that washing, eating and sleeping are incompatible with life in a tent?

The idea that camping involves some kind of hardship is alien to me; my tent is a haven of comfort and peace which provides a welcome retreat from the stresses of the world out-side. When the gales blow and the rain lashes down there is no place more cosy than a tent, no sound more soothing than the patter of rain on canvas, no feeling more secure than that of being safely cocooned from a storm that is raging inches above your head. Okay, so pitching a tent involves a modicum of effort, but even this is not without its little pleasures: the thud of the tent as it drops out of its bag and falls to the ground, the clink of the poles as they slot together, the rustle of the canvas as you smooth it taut over the rigid frame, and finally the moment of fulfilment when, erection complete, you enter the welcoming interior.

In my camping lifetime I have owned tents of all shapes and sizes. Some have been like friends, remaining supportive even under the most trying circumstances; others, frustrating every attempt at a meaningful relationship, have proved formidable opponents. My first tent, a large shed-shaped monstrosity of gossamer-like flimsiness, fell into the latter category. It had no groundsheet, no flysheet, no guys and a slit of a door held together by sewn-on ribbons. In my innocence I tried to erect it at the top of Llanberis Pass in the obligatory howling gale and, ignorant of the possibility of failure, I actually succeeded. When I leapt inside to shelter from the elements the canvas billowed around me like the sail of a storm-tossed boat, giving new meaning to the phrase 'pitching a tent'.

Undeterred, I unfurled a picnic-stained groundsheet on the wet, tussocky grass and sat regally in the middle of it, proud to be a real camper at last. My supposed tentmate, a less adventurous but more sensible soul than me, watched all this from the comfort of our car, enabling me to berate him in his absence for his lack of fortitude. But as I sat there congratulating myself, rain began to seep through the thin cotton above my head and form pools on the groundsheet. Gravity transformed these pools into rivulets that trickled slowly but inexorably towards the lowest point they could find, which just happened to be the depression formed by the seat of my pants. Soon the car had a second occupant and I felt truly chastened.

When I later became a poor student member of the university hillwalking club, club camping equipment served me no better. I recall one bitterly cold winter's night in Glen Nevis when Sandy and I returned from a failed attempt on some ice-bound peak. An icy blast whipped under the sides of our tent (which had no sewn-in groundsheet) and we huddled around the stove for warmth, letting the flames lick our numb fingers. Our morale improved when a pan of risotto, hydrated with water from the swift-flowing Water of Nevis, began to simmer in the beams from our head torches. Alas, the moment was fleeting, for in a nightmarish moment that Sandy never let me forget, my knee inadvertently consigned the contents of the pan to the groundsheet.

Although I now look back on these episodes with nostalgic

fondness I am fiercely loyal to my current tent – a hi-tec, hi-spec geodesic with acres of usable space, sewn-in groundsheet, fly-sheet, guys, porch, front and rear zips, bug-proof netting and internal pockets. The only disadvantage it has over my old tents is that its sewn-in groundsheet is less easily cleaned. In the old days risotto-like substances were relatively easily scraped off a removable groundsheet but... I do not wish to be indelicate here but... twenty years after that episode, less than a few hundred yards from the very same spot in Glen Nevis, my tentmate dis-gorged her evening meal and accompanying rum and blacks into the acres of usable space. It was almost as if she too had been eat-ing risotto. You do not want to know the details, suffice to say the groundsheet proved its waterproofness.

I purchased this tent after a year of other bailing-out episodes with a canvas contraption whose groundsheet had become so threadbare that it was virtually transparent. At first I patched it, then I patched the patches. Gradually the ground-sheet became a patchwork quilt of many colours worthy of artistic exhibition. When even patches failed to stem the tide of rising damp I resorted to placing pebbles and then rocks and boulders under areas of weakness. Before long I was lying in contorted positions as though pinned to the ground in some convulsive seizure. I still have this tent; people I do not like are able to borrow it from me.

Over the years I have acquired a fleet of tents, one for every occasion. I have become a multi-tent household. A geo-desic makes an excellent base camp tent but it is too bulky to carry in comfort. For two-person backpacking step forward Terry the Tortoise, a two-pole crossover with porch named after its shape. One of Terry's most endearing features is his tendency in high winds to deform and flatten, which provides a surprisingly effective means of awakening his occupants. For solitary backpacking I have a lighter single-hoop Goretex, and for single nights out on the move I use a very lightweight trooped bivvy tent that, to the surprise of no-one who has seen it, I call The Coffin. Some might find the interior of The Coffin just a bit too reminiscent of late night horror films in which the hero or heroine is buried alive, but it does provide a surprisingly peaceful night's rest.

There are those who would adopt an even more minimalist approach to nights out in the wild, scorning all notions of canvas for a polythene bivvy bag or even, like Scots drovers of old, nothing but the clothes that cover them. If only modern dress had the warmth, waterproofness and midge-shedding properties of plaid! On occasion the ascetic in me too has taken hold and I have taken to the hills with nothing but a hair shirt and a large poly bag. Fortunately such times have been rare, being directly proportional to the length of time it takes to forget how uncomfortable the last time was.

Rarely is it possible to sleep in a poly bag. The slightest breath of wind is enough to initiate a frenzy of flapping and rustling. The rise and fall of polyurethane above one's face can be maddening. In rain, condensation can be so bad that you might as well sleep outside the bag. In summer, bugs can drive you crazy. Even if there isn't a tarantula-sized arachnid trying to gain access to the inner warmth of your sleeping bag, there's a diarrhoeic owl flying overhead or a large nocturnal creature, glimpsed fleetingly out of the corner of your eye, prowling menacingly in the undergrowth.

A good storm can cure me of the desire to bivouac for in many a long month. I recall one such occasion in the High Pyrenees, when a female companion and I were driven into the shelter of some cottage-sized boulders by a sweeping thunderstorm. We were still cowering from the elements when night fell and the temperature dropped alarmingly. At first we built a fire with wood that had accumulated among the boulders, but the swirling smoke threatened to suffocate us and we decided to extinguish it rather than suffer an untimely and unique end to our hillwalking careers. There remained for warmth my 6ft by 3ft poly bag, which we duly struggled into, lying like trussed turkeys in some bizarre mating ritual. The details of how we spent that terminally uncomfortable, cramp-ridden, shrink-wrapped night I have expunged from memory, but we survived and, although (or perhaps because) movement was impossible, remained (just) good friends.

For the most part I'm happy to leave such adventures to others.

Give me a tent in which to shelter from the elements, a stove for warmth and a sleeping bag in which to snuggle up and I'll be perfectly happy to lie back, content with the world and my place in it, and watch the shadows cast by a lone candle dance on the canvas around me.

My four-season down sleeping bag, a replacement for an old bag that had become so aged and down-free that it could be used on hot summer nights to keep cool is my most trea-

sured item of camping equipment. It has accompanied me around the world and has been there for me in some tight spots. It was there for me when I crawled inside chilled to the bone after a thorough soaking in a Cairngorm blizzard, and it was there for me when the temperature dropped after a Rocky Mountain thunderstorm and the wet tent froze rigid as though stiffened by starch. A good sleeping bag and a stove are what make camping comfortable.

My eyes glaze over with nostalgia at memories of my first stove, a petrol burning monster that belched flames from every nook and cranny and emitted a rising whistling sound as though it were going to achieve take-off velocity at any moment. And one day it did, leaving the ground in one last magnificent death throe before coming to rest black and burned out, fit only to be buried at a safe distance. Needless to say, that stove was not for interior usage, unlike my current efficient but characterless gas stove.

Some campers never use a stove inside a tent for safety reasons and while I appreciate their concerns, there's no way you'll get me brewing up outside on a cold, wet night. As with use of a stove so with all camping activities, care is the secret to the comfort and safety of the endeavour. To this end I insist that anyone sharing my tent obeys the Tent Commandments, as handed down to me on tablets of stone during a high altitude mountaineering expedition. Sample commandments:

Thou shalt not wear boots inside the tent.
Thou shalt stash wet gear at the front of the tent.
Thou shalt light the stove only when there is a pan on top of it.
Thou shalt not steam environmentally unfriendly socks over the stove when wet.

Thou shalt not attempt to walk in thy sleep.
Thou shalt not over-indulge in rum and blacks before retiring.

Anyone breaking a commandment risks excommunication from the tent.

One item of camping equipment I have never owned is a toilet tent. What squeamish mind could have invented that obelisk-shaped incongruity? What did he or she think bushes are for? I once had a girlfriend who refused to camp wild because of her perceived lack of toilet facilities. It may be a Freudian cliché, but she was afraid of snakes. I assured her I had never seen a single snake in all my wanderings around the Highlands, and with therapy she managed to overcome her phobia and became an accomplished camper. In connection with this, female friends assure me that the squatting stance bestowed upon them by nature gives them a closer affinity with the earth, but until there is experimental proof to support such a theory I shall retain the male position.

The only occasion when lack of toilet facilities can prove a nuisance is when nature calls in the middle of a stormy night, when the mere thought of venturing outside makes a sleeping bag seem ever more warm and snug. Human ingenuity has yet to find a solution to this problem, although the advent of roomy tent porches has improved matters no end. Spike Milligan recounts an army solution that involves a length of rubber hose, but the dynamics of the apparatus are complex and it would in any case be of use to only one sex.

Empty cans have the same problem. One hot Highland summer's evening the sky was black and heavy with midges, which battered against the flysheet with a sound like heavy rain. I whiled away the evening idly sipping from a few cans of ale, which had the usual effect. Now there are parts of my body which I would prefer to keep off limits to midges, and so there was no way I was going outside. I solved the problem by refilling the empty cans at regular intervals throughout the night, and am only sorry I can offer no advice to women who find themselves in similar situations.

One way to deal with bugs, be they Scottish midges, Arctic mosquitoes or American no-see-ums, is to light a campfire. As an accompaniment to a winter camp there can be nothing more romantic; there is something primordial and satisfying about sitting on a rock and watching flames lick the cold night air, to say nothing of fire-baked potatoes or toasted marshmallows. Unfortunately the burning of trees for firemaking can no longer be justified either ecologically or environmentally. Even dead branches have their place in the cycle of natural regeneration.

Persuading people to forsake campfires and leave the countryside as they find it is no easy task. With national parks increasingly despoiled by traffic, car parks and building developments, and with a population largely accustomed to greenless cities, it is difficult for people to understand how a mere campfire is going to make much difference. Especially on a cold night. But as the sign says: that which burns never returns. If you really must have a campfire, and I know that some nights were just made for fire-watching, can I suggest the following eco-friendly solution: avoid using local material by taking a bag of sticks with you?

Of course, you could always hang up your tent for the winter, but then you would miss out on the joys of snow camping. To those who have never tried it, camping on snow may seem a cold and uncomfortable activity, but nothing could be further from the truth. There is no easier and more comfortable surface on which to pitch. Pegs penetrate snow like a dream. Once inside the tent the surface of the snow beneath can be moulded through the groundsheet to fit the exact contours of your body. Foam mats provide insulation from the ground and the interior heats up much more quickly and thoroughly than a large multi-roomed house. And the more it snows the cosier it becomes, because snow has excellent insulating properties. Eskimos do not build igloos because they are cold inside.

If I was asked to choose a perfect campsite, however, it would probably be in a less monochrome landscape. It would have no ashen fireplaces left by previous uncaring campers and would look as unspoilt as on the day it was created.

I can see it now in my mind's eye. Beside a gurgling mountain stream is a patch of grass so smooth you would think it had just been mown. Cube-shaped boulders provide wonderful seats. A flat rock ledge jutting out into the stream facilitates access to water. All manner of birds chorus on the branches of riverside trees, which themselves are of all kinds and colours, deciduous and evergreen growing in incongruous proximity. Grassy mounds, carpeted with flowers, block out the wind but not the view. High peaks rise all around, as though this spot and this spot only is the focal point of the entire range.

Not all campsites are so idyllic but even the most unlikely have their compensations. Tussocky grass, for instance, can make you aware of muscles you never knew you had. Hollows that collect water overnight can give the sensation of lying on a waterbed. Sheep droppings are wonderfully pliable and comfortable. The only pitch I can think of that has no redeeming qualities is a tame campsite, erroneously but commonly called an official campsite.

The gathering together of tents to form temporary home-from-home communities in the countryside seems to me to be the antithesis of camping.

Camping for me is an extension of hillwalking and as such is to be conducted preferably as far away from crowds as possible, even if that means carrying a tent to the top of a mountain. When I wake up in the morning it is not the sound of cars, radios and human chatter that I want to hear but the music of the spheres. When I unzip the tent, poke my head out, look around and sniff the air I want to feel at one with the cosmos, as though I were the only person on earth. Memories of such occasions bring a flush of warmth to my cheeks even as I write. Just for that fleeting moment the possibilities that the day might bring seem limitless.

CHAPTER 8

Sex

TO THE ANAPHRODITOUS LAYPERSON (I'm afraid you are going to have to look up some of the words in this chapter) it may seem odd that a book on the joy of hillwalking contains a chapter on sex. Both activities can be pursued with passion but then so can cinema-going, train spotting and reading and you won't find those pursuits discussed here. It is, of course, difficult to watch a film far from an electrical point, spot a train on any mountain except Snowdon or read a book on the move without literally stumbling over your words, so you would expect these activities to be incompatible with hillwalking. But sex is different. Sex is a natural drive that can be combined with most activities, and when combined with hillwalking it can provide some memorable experiences.

To begin with, you cannot get away from the fact that hillwalking is a sensual activity loaded with sexual symbolism. Some mountains have an unmistakable mammillary or phallic appearance, which is sometimes reflected in their names. The Scottish Highlands have numerous examples in the Gaelic language, including Sgurr a' Mhaim (Breast-shaped Peak) in Glen Nevis and monolithic Bod an Deam-hain (Devil's Penis) in the Cairngorms, primly euphemised on most maps to Devil's Point. And how would you like to have a mountain named after a part of your body, as did Mollie Kitchen in 1879? – Mollie's Nipple is a prominent rock peak in the canyonlands of Utah. Let us not also forget that Mount Everest is the largest erection on earth (although some say that size is not everything).

The very activity of hillwalking can be viewed as a sexually symbolic act, beginning with foreplay on the lower slopes and climaxing in the attainment of a peak. Caving has similar symbolisms, and those who indulge in both activities may well be said to swing both ways, usually from a piton. Rock climbers and potholers, of course, need aid to do this and hopefully are fully protected.

Hillwalking improves fitness, muscle-tone and physique. I admit that I have one or two companions whom I would prefer to dress in dull figure-masking anoraks if only to prevent visual pollution of the hill, but overall a mountain top is as good a place as any to meet attractive people. On the continent the beautiful people even take to the hill dressed in designer clothes, and sometimes not much of that. In France some degree of undress is almost *de rigeur* during the summer months. Complete nudity is less common, for reasons I am sure I need not go into; hillwalking in such a state is recommended only to those who are into urtication or the like.

Naked rock climbing, on the other hand, does rear its head from time to time on crags in Australia, North America and other hot places. In a way it is surprising that it is not more common because, after all, is rock climbing not merely a form of frottage? The naked variety is an almost exclusively male preserve and is often dismissed as an example of male exhibitionism, but perhaps there are some jamming techniques of which I am unaware. As for naked ice climbing, there are many first ascents still to be made in this field owing to the fact that the low temperature normally makes additional jamming techniques impractical.

Unless you are of an acrobatic inclination, sexual activity in its narrowest sense may seem to be as incompatible with hillwalking as any other concurrent physical activity, but in its wider sense it raises a number of interesting possibilities for those who have drives in both areas. I refer here to a sex drive in its physiological sense, not as a Sunday afternoon vehicular alternative to hillwalking when the high tops are in cloud.

As an example of the cross-fertilisation between the two areas of human endeavour, exercise is known to both stimulate the sexual drive and at the same time place one in a relaxed and receptive frame of mind. Beware too much exercise, however, as this can be both counter-productive and counter-reproductive. It is one thing to have your sex drive stimulated but quite another to work up enough energy to satisfy it when you are exhausted after a long day on the hill. I hope such days are rare for you.

Perhaps it is the volatile relationship between sex and exercise that fuels the argument about whether sex before exercise improves or diminishes athletic performance, and perhaps this lies at the heart of bar-room debates about whether one's partner should accompany one on weekend trips. Does one variety of mounting enhance or detract from the other and, if so, which should have priority? Perhaps you should get the next round in first.

I confess that any form of sexual activity before hillwalking is out of the question as far as I am concerned. When the alarm goes off for an early morning start my body is barely up to crawling out of bed never mind anything else. It normally requires a pit stop for an egg butty followed by the sight of my intended mountain looming through the windscreen before I can even take the matchsticks out of my eyelids. Don't you just hate people who are wide awake first thing in the morning and insist on conversing all the way to the hill?

Sex after hillwalking is probably the ideal sequence of events, provided that the reason you are laid out in the missionary position is not exhaustion. And as a way of passing an evening in a tent it certainly beats 'I Spy'. Solo campers can always find their own amusement, and in connection with this, note that recent research has shown that no amount of self-amusement will affect your balance on the hill.

With regard to sex after hillwalking, I trust you will keep it to yourself when I tell you that I owe my first sexual experience to a day on the hill. The mountain of fond memory was Aonach Eagach, the narrow ridge that bounds the north side of Glen Coe. Some hillwalkers are able to trot along this ridge as though it were a pavement flanked by nothing more vertiginous than a kerbstone, while others would not dare to tackle its pinnacles and drop-offs without at least one spare pair of brown corduroy breeches in the rucksack.

On the day in question I was undertaking my umpteenth traverse of the ridge and had become so blasé about it that my familiarity with the moves could easily have been taken for a competence that some members of the opposite sex find attractive. Such was the case with one inexperienced female member of our party who lost her nerve half-way along and froze motionless in mid-stride. While the rest of the party went on ahead I offered to stay behind and help her. I had to coax her every step of the way, placing her hands and feet on holds and talking her across difficult moves. Later I discovered that her inexperience stretched only as far as hillwalking. She was very grateful. But nowhere near as much as I was. I have been back to Aonach Eagach many times since, but despite much loitering with intent my services have never again been required.

Some authorities profess that sex during a hill walk is the best combination of the two activities, and this theory dove-tails neatly with surveys showing that The Great Outdoors is a popular location for sexual pursuits, if only in imagination. Lack of privacy may sometimes pose a problem, but it is usually possible to find a secluded place, such as behind a boulder, before the urge passes. And if all else fails you can always head for the nearest cloud. In my experience it is rarely necessary to seek out a bathykolpian cleft in which to conceal yourself – a wide-open plateau with all-round vision is sufficient and affords a better view afterwards. And when your ear is close to the ground it is amazing from how far you can hear the sound of approaching boots. Note also that if the earth moves at anything greater than force 5 on the Richter scale it is unlikely to be the result of your technique and perhaps you had better get out of there fast.

Broad plateau summits make attractive locations. I can rec-ommend, for example, the summit of Windy Hill the highest point on the island of Bute, and several tops in the Cairngorms (I refrain from naming them in order to deter voyeurs). Any remote place is a good candidate. Unfrequented lochsides, warmed by sparkling sun and lapped by rippling water, are espe-cially romantic. If you want to join the mile-high club, however, you will have to go abroad. The nearest spot where Brits can get their membership is in the French Jura, where the Crêt de la Neige reaches 5,653ft, but I know of no travel firm offering weekend trips for such a purpose.

All that we might reasonably ask of a mountain in support of sexual activity is comfortable terrain, and in truth the hills abound with suitable spots. For prone positions it is usually possible to find a horizontal plane of smooth rock or grass. Sloping terrain requires much more energy input and can only be recommended if you use a rock or a tree stump for purchase. On the steep forested slopes of Ben Venue in the Trossachs my partner and I once only managed to maintain momentum with the aid of both a tree stump and a well-positioned ice axe. The truth can now be told that it was this incident that I referred to in a previous guidebook when I related that 'much fun can be had among the tree-girt crags above the lochside.'

Woodlands provide cover, soft ground and a variety of accompanying sounds, but beware the local insect population and watch out for pine needles, which can be murder on the knees. As for boulder ruckles and tussocky grass, these are suitable for advanced positions only. Snow would provide a perfect, malleable surface were it not of a temperature that tends to shrivel the sex drive and its male apparatus. And note that any attempt to consummate a relationship on granular snow is likely to dampen your enthusiasm for sitting glissades for at least a couple of days afterwards. There may be rock jocks who swear by chalk bags as winter warmers but personally when it becomes cold enough to snap an icicle in two I restrict my amorous activities to the inside of a tent. A tent has the benefit of privacy and the advantage that it can be pre-warmed by a stove, but do remember to turn off the stove before proceeding. Let the following cautionary tale be a warning to all.

It happened in the Llanberis Pass at the foot of Snowdon. We were camped beside a roadside crag which, because of cloud on the high tops, was festooned with rock climbers. Safe and secure in our tent, my partner and I were happy to take a rest day and pass the time in activities that do not normally require the wearing of boots. Unfortunately we omitted to turn off the stove and somehow (we were too preoccupied to notice how) it got knocked over.

The first evidence that all was not well was a burning hole in the front corner of the tent. A fresh breeze fanned the burgeoning fire and almost before we could move a sheet of flame whipped over our heads with an audible whoosh. In the space of a few seconds the whole tent apart from the groundsheet had disappeared from around us, leaving only smouldering boots that had been airing under the flysheet to indicate the passing of the firestorm. I often wonder how this must have appeared to the nearby climbers, who would have seen a ball of windblown flame rising across their crag and two puzzled people lying naked on the ground. I jumped to my feet, dazed by the suddenness of the incident but aware that this very public spot was no place for a naked, upstanding member of the hillwalking community. We retreated to our car.

There are some who would read significance into this incident. There are others who are embarrassed by such matters and would prefer them not to be talked about. There are still others who would have dark powers of retribution rain down on those who take off their boots for anything save the bursting of blisters. To them I offer some words of Anais Nin, which seem to me to apply equally well to sexual activity, hillwalking and life in general: 'Oh, it is sweet to be contented, but it is far more thrilling to be ever dissatisfied and reaching out, for who knows how far and where a great thirst may lead you.'

CHAPTER 9

Maps and Guidebooks

'I AM TOLD THAT THERE are people who do not care for maps,'
wrote Robert Louis Stevenson, 'and I find it hard to believe.'
Me too, but I suppose I should expect no more in a world
where there are people who do not even like climbing mountains.

What a wonderful piece of work is a map. When I take one
at random from the shelf and let its concertina-like folds slip
through my fingers, a frisson of excitement runs down my
spine as impressions of mountains, valleys, forests and lakes
dance across my vision. When it falls open at some random
fold my heart skips a beat as details of crags, streams, paths
and spot heights fight for my attention. And then the climac-
tic moment when the mapmaker's stylised etchings crystallise
into meaning and a vision of the landscape floods the mind. If
imagination is a characteristic that distinguishes us from the
animals, then surely map reading is one of the highest pursuits
of mankind.

Modern British maps spoil us with their coruscating cartography. You have only to cast an eye over early maps of Britain,
such as Johan Blaeu's 1654 atlas or William Roy's 1755 survey
of Scotland, to see how much we have to thank today's
Ordnance Survey and private mapmakers such as Bartholomew
and Harvey. It is astonishing how much detail the old uncon-
toured, uncoloured maps seem to lack. It was not until 1774,
when the Astronomer Royal and his team went to Schiehallion
to estimate the mass of the earth, that the wonderful idea of
drawing lines to connect points of equal height to form contours

occurred to one of the survey party, Dr Charles Hutton. Colour was added later along with techniques such as shading, hachuring and layering to highlight relief, resulting in the masterpieces of representation that we know today.

I sometimes wonder what more we could ask of our mapmakers. Some indication of rock type, perhaps – nothing as scientifically precise as on a geological map but enough to distinguish, for example, between loose quartzite and good solid granite. Even more useful would be some indication of the rock's magnetic properties, so that one would know to be wary of the compass on mountain ranges like the Cuillin of Skye. Symbols for differing terrain, as on orienteering maps, would enable us to distinguish hillsides of springy turf from entangling bracken. On the other hand maybe some things are best not foreseen. Perhaps a perfect map would diminish the thrill of discovery that adds so much to a day on the hill.

This is not to say that there is no room for improvement. There are two features that I would campaign to see re-introduced on OS maps: the hill shading and layer tints that used to adorn old one-inch-to-one-mile Tourist Maps. The light and dark brown shading on the old Tourist Map of Lorn and Lochaber throws the narrow ridges of Aonach Eagach and Carn Mor Dearg into sharp and eye-catching relief. The layer tints on the old Peak District Tourist Map are shamelessly evocative, the land rising from a tame green to a lovely golden brown over 1,700ft. The old Cairngorm Tourist Map is even more beautiful the land over 3,000ft standing out in brilliant purple, rising to an almost pristine white, as if resembling snow, at the 4,000ft summits of Braeriach and Ben Macdui.

We tend to take the accuracy of British maps for granted, but it doesn't take much more than a short stroll on foreign soil to make you realise how much loving work has gone into them. In Scandinavia it is quite common to be denied a seemingly easy summit by an abrupt rock face not shown on the map. In Canada and the USA the vastness of the wilderness makes large-scale maps generally impracticable, and those that do exist lack topographic detail. Other countries have surveyed their mountains for military purposes only, and the resulting maps sometimes seem to bear no relation to the land at all. Sardinian maps, for example, are available only from the Italian Instituto Geografico Militare in Florence and as aids to hillwalking are best read with an air of detached amusement. I do not mean these examples to imply criticism, for on maps of countries whose mountains are higher, wilder and less explored than our own we should not expect to find the same level of cartographic detail.

Even OS maps have their inaccuracies. One I am particularly fond of involves a Highland loch that has streams flowing out of both ends, eventually to meet some miles distant – a hydrological curiosity worthy of an Escher etching and one I am reluctant to identify in case the OS should decide to correct it. My only real complaint, however, as a hillwalker living in Scotland, concerns the misspelling, misunderstanding, misuse and misplacement of Gaelic names by nineteenth-century English mapmakers. Some names are so absurd that they make any attempt at a direct pronunciation ludicrous. Stob Diamh of Ben Cruachan, for example, should be spelled Stob Damh (pronounced *Daff* meaning Stag Peak). Coire Domdain in Kintail should be spelled Coire Domhain (pronounced *Doe-in*, meaning Deep Corrie). It's enough to make any Highlander rise up in arms once again against the Sassenachs.

Nineteenth-century mapmakers also bequeathed a legacy of trigonometrical pillars that angers some modern conservationists, who consider the construction of these alien hilltop artefacts to have been an act of vandalism. Others, including myself, prefer to view them as part of our cultural heritage, along with other mountain edifices such as cairns and dykes. I admit that I would consider an outburst of similar construction activity today to be unsupportable, but there is something comforting about the presence of a trig pillar at the top of a hill; placing a hand on one has for me always been a sign of a successful ascent and I'd miss that. Let us not judge the mapmakers of yesteryear by the mores of today. Of the 6,173 trig pillars in existence, 4,904 have now been made redundant by modern satellite positioning technology; I applaud moves by the OS to allow interested groups to 'adopt' those no longer needed.

If you should ever doubt the value of an accurate map, try walking in unfamiliar territory without one, as I had to on Sardinia when none was available. Our proposed coastal backpack seemed straightforward enough (we had only to keep the sea to our left), but on the second day out we became hopelessly lost on a 2,000ft slope of entangling maquis from which it took a further two days to extricate ourselves. That incident gave me a new respect for maps.

Of course, a map, like a book, is useless unless you can read it, but rarely can so much pleasure be gained from so little effort. At one point in my life I found myself teaching mapreading to primary schoolchildren, and I still recall the growing sense of wonder on their faces as they began to realise that a two-dimensional sketch could depict a three-dimensional world. They mastered map symbols relatively easily but contour lines proved more of a problem. There was a look of disbelief in their eyes as I explained how closely grouped contour lines indicated steep ground, while those wider apart indicated easy-angled slopes. They gaped in astonishment as I showed, with the help of photographs, how the lines bulged out to show a spur and curved in to show a valley. Some had difficulty in distinguishing the two, as I still do on maps that omit drainage and contour heights.

How much more I wanted to tell them. About how to detect glaciated U-shaped valleys, direction of river flow, plateaus and narrow ridges, corries and passes. About true north, magnetic north and grid north. About how to use a compass to determine direction of travel, identify a mountain or calculate your position by backbearings. Or even how to determine intervisibilty between two points, calculate ground distance as opposed to map distance or conduct an expanding spiral search. Such advanced activities would perhaps have been beyond them, but I bet they would have found them more interesting than arithmetic.

Maps have such exciting possibilities. As well as their functional utility they are without peer as a catalyst to the imagination. Although I have walked in the Scottish Highlands for many years, I never cease to be amazed at how much I can still learn by studying maps of them. In my early hillwalking days the old one-inch-to-one-mile series was my trusty guide to the hills, and I still have a treasured set of these maps, annotated with Munros, wild campsites and other features. To most hillwalkers they are now no more than collector's items, consigned to the cartographic scrapheap by metrication, but they will always be dear to me. Although dog-eared and musty, weathered, abraded and worn at the folds, they will always be redolent of early days spent exploring what to me was a brand new world.

I still study maps of the Highlands, now seeking out new and interesting routes up familiar peaks. While others search for the easiest way to bag a Munro I explore in imagination some previously unsuspected spur or valley that will provide a more appealing line to the top. While others check out official long distance footpaths I'm wondering if it would be possible to walk the watershed from Central Scotland to the Pentland Firth. I lay out all the maps on the carpet. I draw the line of the route. It's a huge expedition. The section east of Ullapool, where a maze of lochans drain to all points of the compass, looks like a fascinating navigational challenge. Of course, unusually for British hillwalks, it would be the driest expedition imaginable and I'd have to make side trips down to the nearest water...

A few years back the advent of the mountain bike sent me scuttling back to familiar maps to seek out yet another set of routes. Now it was possible to tackle mountains via remote, previously overlong approaches, cycling in and leaving the bicycle at the foot of the ascent (to avoid damaging ecologically fragile mountainsides). More than this, the map revealed a whole new set of possibilities that I had previously overlooked. The Highland landscape contained more than mountains, it was criss crossed by a network of old cattle droving routes, military roads, whisky routes, ancient Pictish roads and many others. The map suddenly showed me ways of exploring the Highlands that I had never considered before. It was a revelation.

Maps do that to me. I can happily pore over them for hours. Who knows what new insight into the landscape might be gained or what previously unconsidered hillwalk might present itself for my inspection? Sometimes I unfold a past summer's Didier-Richard or USGS and retrace routes of fond memory across the Alps or Rockies. And if you really want to keep me quiet give me a map of some place I've never been, like Tasmania. After months of study since being given a map of this island as a Christmas present I can now tell you the best approach route to the Labyrinth in Cradle Mountain – Lake St. Clair National Park, while the very thought of a traverse of the Western Arthurs has me leafing wistfully though round-the-world air fares. Another recent addition to my esoteric collection is a map of the island of Reunion off Madagascar, should you ever want to know the best way of tackling the Piton des Neiges.

Some prefer not to plan in this way and see what happens on the ground, and I have every sympathy with this point of view, notwithstanding the fact that Safetyman would have us leave details of our every step with some authority or other. I have always felt a great affinity with Eric Shipton, the great Himalayan explorer who pioneered the route to Everest from the Nepal side and who was passionately attracted to places he described as *Blank on the Map*, the wonderful title of his 1943 book of explorations.

I met Shipton in his later years – a marvellous man whose exploratory enthusiasm remained forever undimmed. I day-dream about following in his footsteps and exploring the uncharted regions of the world, but while, like most hillwalkers, my sorties abroad are limited by the demands of a job, I am happy to have a map to help me plan the trip. There is also the additional pleasure of anticipation that mapreading brings. Planning may not be better than doing but put me in a padded cell, slot a map of Reunion Island through the grille, let me wander in imagination among the cloudswept peaks of the Indian Ocean and for a while at least I'll want for nothing.

While most hillwalkers would at least admit to the useful-ness of maps, not everyone likes guidebooks. Critics complain that they encourage ill-equipped people onto the hill and advertise the countryside to those who would otherwise stay away, thereby increasing environmental pressure. It turns out that those who complain the loudest, however, are often those who simply want to keep the hills to themselves.

Wild land is part of our national heritage and if a guide-book can promote a better appreciation of it then I'm all for it. Only by encouraging people to know their natural environ-ment will the future of the planet be secured, and from a humanistic standpoint what better antidote than hillwalking could there be to the alienation felt by many people in twentieth-century urban life? In an increasingly populated and industrialised world it is not surprising that increasing numbers of people want to experience wild places. If you want to spread the load on the countryside and encourage people not to abuse the privilege of being able to explore it, then stop building roads that reduce the amount of wild land available and stop building visitor centres that serve as focal points. There are many ways of combatting overcrowding without withholding knowledge of what the countryside has to offer. Let us have laws and guidebooks that open up the land to all.

Good guidebooks are both informative and entertaining, but making them so is no easy task – information obtained from exhaustive research soon has a habit of becoming obsolete. And no matter how often the book is proof-read by however many people, at least one embarrassing error will always creep in, be it a misplaced digit in a grid reference number or specifying right instead of left (an error in one of my guidebooks that people still point out to me with glee). In defence I list the possible existence of such errors as one of the joys of reading guidebooks – they make the reader pay close attention to the text and their detection gives him a feeling of self-satisfaction at his superiority to the author.

There are good guidebooks and bad ones, but the best usually stand out like an 8,000 metre peak and make the whole enterprise worthwhile. Reading about mountains may be a poor substitute for climbing them, but there are worse ways of spending a long winter's evening than reliving past ascents, comparing one's own experiences with those of the author and planning the trips of tomorrow.

My creaking bookshelves harbour an eclectic collection of guidebooks. Pocket paperbacks extolling the virtues of various

British mountain regions sit side by side with dusty ancient tomes cataloguing early Alpine explorations. Slim leaflets describing short trips in this or that glen stand defiantly beside guides to the world's great mountain ranges. Just to hold such books in my hands makes my mouth water for the hills. Even the spines, whose design alone now makes a book instantly recognisable to me, have the power of evocation. As I run my fingers along them like a Tibetan prayer wheel, it is as though I am making my own supplication to the mountains.

My two current favourite guidebooks border on the esoteric. One is the only walking book currently available on Sardinia, an idiosyncratic but irresistible Italian work that combines walking, rock-climbing and caving routes. I love its presumption that if you go to Sardinia to do anything other than lie on a beach you must by default want to do all of these other activities. The other is a book on the Tatra Mountains written in Polish, an impossibly difficult language that makes the text virtually useless to an English speaker even with the aid of a dictionary. Yet I find myself leafing through it with excitement, mesmerised by the meaningless prose and the hidden solutions it contains to so many mountain mysteries. It is also a good book to leave lying around accidentally when impressionable acquaintances drop by.

No guidebook, however, will ever mean as much to me as my first: a guidebook to Snowdonia produced by the Youth Hostels Association in 1961. Alongside evocative sketches and descriptions of mountains with magical Welsh names such as Yr Wyddfa and Cnicht, it included an extract from H.V. Morton's *In Search of Wales* that was instrumental in initiating my passion for the hills: 'the mist moved thickly and the wind came over the top of Snowdon to an eerie moan.' I wanted to hear that wind.

CHAPTER 10

Food and a Bit of Literary Criticism

JAM SANNIES NEVER TASTE SO good as at the top of a mountain. It's almost worth struggling to the top just for the pleasure of eating them. As you delve into the depths of your rucksack and search for the soggy morass squashed beneath layers of spare clothing and sundry sharp pointed items of equipment that you didn't mean to bring with you (and no wonder you haven't been going too well), you just know they're going to taste like manna. When you packed them carefully in a supposedly uncrushable corner of your sack you wondered if you would ever really want them and so you packed a few bars of chocolate and other goodies as well, but now you kneel down and give thanks for your foresight. And the more disintegrated they are, the more they have to be oozed into your mouth through sticky fingers, the better they taste.

No matter whether the bread is brown or white, wheat or rye, leavened or unleavened. No matter whether it's spread with butter or margarine. Maybe for you it's not jam, maybe it's peanut butter, Marmite, cheese, caviar or plain salt and vinegar. Perhaps it's followed by a dessert of Kendal mint cake, a chocolate biscuit or a home-made fruit bar whose secret recipe you would not pass on to future generations even if you were found lying broken, bloody and breathing your last breath at the foot of a cliff. The mouth waters at the mere cataloguing of such delicacies.

For lubrication give me fresh mountain stream water every time. You can keep your flasks of hot tea, coffee and chocolate, and you can especially keep your cans of sickly, foul-tasting Fizzade. If I should pass by the cairn where you sit cradling a steaming mug while the tempest whirls impotently around you, please, curb your admirable desire to offer me a drink. I know you mean well and I don't wish to give offence by refusing your offer, but hot or cold, rain or shine, a few handfuls of springwater are all I crave. Long may the high mountain streams of the Scottish Highlands, unlike those of the USA, remain uncontaminated by giardia and safe to drink.

If you find this diet lacking in culinary imagination I can only blame it on my working-class upbringing, but I remain unrepentant. I know what I like. If you want to prance around the hills in Sound of Music fashion with picnic baskets full of provolone and profiteroles then that's up to you. Personally I aspire to the régime of Scottish shepherds of yore who made porridge once a week poured it into a drawer to solidify and then hacked daily pieces off it to stuff in their pockets for the hill. In Scotland a sandwich is still called a piece. While climbing the south face of Annapurna in 1970 Don Whillans found himself alone and without food in a high camp until Scot Dougal Haston reached him. And what was the sole delicacy that, much to Don's chagrin, Dougal had brought with him? A poly bag full of oats. Now that's class.

On the continent the eating habits of the average British hillwalker would be looked upon with bewilderment. Because the Alps are higher than British mountains a day's walk of a few thousand feet will take you not to a mountain top but to an Alpine hut, and this is objective enough for most hillwalkers, for whom the ascent is in any case a mere preliminary to the main event of the day – lunch. French huts especially can sometimes seem like nothing more than high-altitude restaurants bulging with diners. No French hillwalker would last the day without a lunch of several courses that takes at least an hour to eat. The huts even sell alcohol, gateaux and other goodies to augment the feast.

The best time to visit an Alpine hut is in the morning, after any climbers staying overnight have left for their peak but before the hordes of day walkers arrive. After a dawn start from the road-end a late breakfast of *oeufs plats*, served piping hot in the frying pan on the terrace of a superbly sited hut, is one of the joys of Alpine hillwalking. And there is no better place from which to plan the rest of the day as the sun warms the surrounding peaks and the glaciers glisten and beckon.

How different are the spartan huts of Eastern Europe, where often the only sustenance obtainable is a lukewarm herbal tea that tastes like liquid sawdust. Owing to the popularity of the huts and their lack of seating accommodation, this insipid liquid often has to be drunk standing in a cold, plain, crowded room. I applaud the community spirit that this breeds among the siblinghood of hillwalkers, but visiting Alpinists must soon get nostalgic for the fleshpots of home.

If the French climb to their mountain huts to eat lunch, the Norwegians spend the night in theirs in preparation for a breakfast bash. As they stagger sleepy-eyed from their bunks a gargantuan feast greets their eyes – the famous smorgasbord: tables full of cereals, cold meats, pâtés, breads and biscuits, fish, cheeses, fruit, hot and cold drinks... In at least one hut you can buy a postcard of the gastronomic event as a memento. There are some fine mountains in Norway, but my most vivid memories of a hut-to-hut walk there are of tables creaking with food at a time of day when man (well, this man anyway) was surely meant to be abed.

My most memorable mountain eating experience, however, occurred elsewhere in Europe, when I had to make a day trip into another country to fetch the groceries. We were camped in a high Alpine valley on the French side of the Franco-Italian border, from where the quickest way to reprovision was to cross the pass that formed the border and descend to the nearest Italian village. In searing heat we came down out of the mountains with a fistful of lire and arrived at the village's one store just before it closed for the afternoon siesta. In the few minutes available to us (and it required a determined profligacy) we managed to part company with every single lira in our possession, and we hauled back to our high mountain camp on the other side of the border a treasure trove of delicacies that turned the next few days' meals into gourmet extravaganzas.

Only once have I been better fed on a mountain and that was at 11,664ft (3,555m) in the top cable-car station of Mount Teide on Tenerife. Most visitors reach this point by cable-car, looking cold and bored and wishing they were still on the beach. But true hillwalkers take the wonderful route up by the Montana Blanca, climbing through a lunar landscape and past an ice cave that can be entered by ladder, and as reward for their endeavours they find themselves at a mirage-like establishment that offers a menu of waffles with strawberry jam and cream washed down by hot chocolate laced with cognac. Perhaps I need to rethink my diet of jam sannies and water.

Britain too is not without its mountain eating establishments. In Victorian times you could dine in relative splendour in the observatory at the summit of Ben Nevis, and even today there are ski-slope cafés in Scotland and a seasonal mountain-top café on Snowdon. I once took my long-suffering hillwalking companion Wendy up Snowdon on a day of low cloud when I assured her that unfortunately the café would be closed. And so it was only fair that I should be severely reprimanded when we arrived cold and cashless at the summit to find the café open and an array of tempting delicacies on offer. Suitably sullen, we sought somewhere to sulk out of sight and smell of the café, and it was at this point that I dangled

before Wendy's eyes a £10 note that I had mischievously secreted in an inside pocket. The look on her face was worth the beating I received, and the ensuing spending spree ensured my rehabilitation.

I attempted to pull a similar kind of surprise on another companion with whom I walked the long coastal route from Glen Brittle to Loch Coruisk on Skye. We stopped for lunch beside the loch, basking on baked gabbro slabs while we cooled our feet in a waterslide. With the panache of a conjuror I pulled from my sack a large, heavy can of juicy peaches, which I had carried secretly and without complaint in anticipation of this moment. Alas, I had forgotten a can opener, and after assorted rocks had failed to make more than a dent in the recalcitrant receptacle I had to carry it all the way back to Glen Brittle again.

On backpacking trips there are limits to the amount of food that can be carried and if, like me, you are about as able to live off the land as the average goldfish, dehydrated food is the only solution. But why does most of it have the look, consistency and taste of mud? Am I the only one who suspects that all those brightly coloured, exotically labelled pouches contain the very same mucus-like substance? A few days on the stuff is enough to make anyone fantasise about jam sannies.

My most pitiful experience with dehydrated food occurred towards the end of a Pyrenean backpacking trip, when all that remained in the larder were a few chunks of unseemly grey texturised vegetable protein and a packet of insipid soup in which to marinate them. Every single mouthful of that horrendous meal was a digestive challenge.

On another occasion my digestive system embarrassingly failed to meet the challenge. I was halfway up the 4,500ft ascent from the bottom of the Grand Canyon to the rim and had stopped at the oasis of Garden Creek springs in debilitating heat to rehydrate a colourful packet of peaches and cream pie. Anxious to be on my way, I ate it before it was fully rehydrated. The consequences were predictable and less than dignified. On the interminable and crowded series of switchbacks that led back up to the canyon rim there were several occasions when my body begged to be allowed to explode and I was forced to sprint for a rare sequestered blind corner with a speed that belied my exhaustion.

Such are the vagaries of memory that in retrospect it is possible to recall such experiences with humour, especially when they are immediately followed by a return to the fleshpots of civilisation. The first regular meal after days or weeks in the wilderness makes any prior discomfort bearable. I remember as if it were yesterday...

At the end of a two-week backpacking trip in the Rockies I fetch up in Pinedale, a sleepy cow-town on the high plains of Wyoming; population 1,000. It has a general store, several shops, motels and gas stations, a taxidermy receiving station that advertises itself with a sketch of an improbably contented black bear, an Aladdin's cave of a sporting goods store, Papa Joe's Indian artefacts store and the Wrangler café. At Papa Joe's you can buy a T-shirt that bears the legend 'Where the hell's Pinedale'?

After surviving on a diet of muesli, crackers, cup-a-soup and various unidentifiable dehydrated substances I make a beeline for the Wrangler café and a feast I have been drooling over in anticipation for days. I begin with the tastiest cream cheese bagel that has ever been toasted and follow with a grilled wholewheat bread cheese sandwich and fries, flawlessly cooked in their skins. The feast reaches its climax with home-made blueberry pie à la mode lubricated by a single bottle of Budweiser. For half an hour America has never seemed so beautiful. Then I double up with stomach cramp.

In the heart of the French Pyrenees, dwarfed by vast tree-clad mountainsides and bypassed by the road to Spain, lies the seemingly deserted village of Porta. The ramshackle stone houses with their pretty red-tiled roofs cook in the early afternoon sun. Only a mongrel dog braves the stupefying heat as it skittles from one place to another, bent on some canine errand. Otherwise there is not a breath of movement.

But wait! Puffs of dust on the shimmering hillside betray the approach of two figures. Their heavily laden backpacks and raw, peeling faces indicate that they have been out for some time. They arrive at Porta in the early stages of heat exhaustion, their throats parched, their saliva long ago dried up. It is some time before the various buildings distinguish themselves in the glaring brightness, but then an unlikely apparition takes form before their eyes – a subterranean grocery.

Wooden steps lead down beneath a house into a cool dark dungeon stocked with the stuff of a backpacker's dreams. Shelf upon shelf is piled high with tinned fruit, biscuits, confectionery and cans of juice that scream 'Drink me' in English. On a counter stands a shank of boiled ham and beside it lean sacks of fresh root vegetables. One dusty sack, miracle of miracles, contains stale French bread. The backpackers grab at the loaves. A grizzled old shopkeeper shufffles across the floor in footwear that was old when he was a boy and has to physically restrain them.

The two backpackers emerge laden into the searing sunlight. They succumb to an ant-infested spot of ground beneath a shady tree and pillage their purchases. Swigs of milk, orange juice and beer slip sweetly past cracked lips, gulped down alternately to maximise the relish of their differing tastes. In Norse mythology the hero Thor had to drain the Horn of Plenty in three draughts, and he nearly succeeded despite the fact that the end of the horn reached into the ocean. On this day the backpackers would have outdrunk Thor.

But there is a price to pay. The ensuing few hours, during which they struggle bloated into the mosquito-ridden mountains of Spain, burdened with tins of food and a six-pack of French beer, are amongst the most penitential they have ever experienced on the hill. They spend the next day holed up in the tent recovering, too ill even to face the beer. The next day again one of them half-buries the six-pack beneath a pyramid of stones in the centre of the trail – a dubious gift for the next hillwalker along. Yes, this was long before the days of conservational awareness and 'pack it in – pack it out' philosophy and yes, I was that backpacker.

Ten years later I disappear into the wastes of the Norwegian Jotunheimen, a region of inhospitable terrain and stunning beauty. Staffed mountain huts ease the burden of food haulage and bread migrates from breakfast tables to bulging anorak pockets. There are a few parts of the Jotunheimen that are so remote, however, that they contain only unstaffed huts and here, in a landscape as wild as you could wish for, is one of the world's great food caches.

The hut stands in a stark glacial valley between jagged rock peaks. Inside are stocks of packaged and canned food, replenished by helicopter at regular intervals. The food is bought on trust; there is a price list and you leave the appropriate krone in the envelope provided. The system is a wonderful tribute to the honesty of Norwegians and visiting backpackers; if only it were possible elsewhere.

As I sift through cans of meat and vegetables and packets of mashed potato my eye catches an unexpected delicacy that makes my heart skip a beat – a packet of porridge oats. Suddenly I'm in love. It's one of those things you can't explain. I'm not averse to porridge in the way that Whillans was but neither am I a porridge freak. Yet at this precise moment in my life a bowl of porridge is all I need to achieve satori.

Unfortunately a single bowlful is not enough to satisfy my craving – the glutinous contents go down almost unnoticed. Two large bowlfuls later my appetite for the gooey grey stuff is still undiminished. How much more I eat I shall later never remember nor want to remember. I stop eating when there are no oats left and then I sleep. The next morning I awake in abdominal agony and there occurs a series of events whose precise details are best not committed to print. Suffice to say that the following two days, during which I have to drag my stooped body out to civilisation to catch a plane, are amongst the most purgatorial of my life.

Yet still I do not repent. If you refuse a joyful experience because of potentially hurtful consequences then you will miss out on many of the joys of life. This is as true of food as it is of relationships. That way lies asceticism, cynicism and vegetation. Far better to remain vulnerable, take chances and live life to the full. In some things it is best not to learn.

The idea that we go through life learning from experiences does not accord with reality. The notion of life as a novel, with a plot that continuously evolves, is a Victorian fantasy nourished by portraits of contrived lives in Dickensian fiction. When *A Christmas Carol* was first published in instalments and shipped across the Atlantic to the USA, immigrants from the old country would line the quaysides hungry for the latest news of their heroine. 'Is Little Nell dead?' they would enquire. That first soap opera now has its televisual counterparts and the myth of life as a series of linked plot developments continues to be propagated in the public consciousness.

My experiences with food and other matters tell me differently. Life is rather a series of short stories. Like good authors we keep repeating the same theme with variations. Every experience merely adds another layer. As the philosopher said (and

I paraphrase): 'Life is an onion.' Patterns emerge and are repeated. Every day I am born anew to gorge myself on porridge and climb mountains and wonder yet again: Why am I doing this? May I never learn!

CHAPTER II

Flora and Fauna

IF YOU'RE EXPECTING THIS chapter to contain an informative discourse on the wondrous ways in which flora and fauna enhance a day on the hill then you're in for a disappointment. To be frank, everything I know about flora could be etched into the adze-head of an ice axe. Don't get me wrong – I love flowers and trees and have even been known to give the odd fungus and fern a passing glance. It's just that I'm hopeless with names.

Some people have problems with names of people or places, with me it's flora. I can tell you the name of everyone who accompanied me to the summit of Ben Nevis in 1966, and of every peak and pass I crossed on my journey through the Queyras twenty years later, but all little yellow flowers with five petals look like buttercups to me. You can try to teach me the difference between a hairy buttercup and a woolly buttercup until you're as blue as a Bonnington after an enforced bivouac at 8,000 meters, but I'm afraid it will make little difference.

I know I should be ashamed of myself but what can I do? Over the years I have collected a shelf-full of books on the subject in an effort to obtain botanical enlightenment, and I have taken to the hill with enormous field guides whose weight neither the human nor rucksack frame was designed to carry. All to no avail. Even with book in hand and knelt in intimate proximity to an offending growth, its precise designation remains inaccessible to me – either it refuses to match any picture in the book or it matches several. Perhaps there is something wrong with my floral recognition system, although it seems to have functioned perfectly well in childhood. At school I won first prize in a competition to see who could collect the most different kinds of wild flowers. My teacher wrote on my school report that I was interested in nature study, whereas what I was really interested in was prizes.

Am I the only one who skips the flora chapter in a hillwalking guidebook? Am I the only one who squirms when a pretentious writer, in the middle of a prosaic description of a walk, digresses to extol in purple prose the virtues of the *saxifraga stellaris* or the *cardaminopsis petrea*? It's not that I wish to knock botanical knowledge. I'm sure that knowing that a plant environment is rich in *pedicularis sylvatica* (lousewort) is of enormous concern to some people and extremely useful from an ecological viewpoint. But not to me.

I'm quite content to view my flora as a mass undifferentiated phenomenon. This doesn't mean that I appreciate it any less – I'm as moved as the next person by a hillside of swaying colour or even by a dull excuse for a plant clinging to life in some gloomy rock niche. But I don't need to pigeonhole the experience. In the same way that a trivia quiz is more enjoyable when you don't know all the answers, my botanical ignorance never ceases to bring me the joy of the unexpected.

I have the same problem with trees that I do with flowers. Real-life specimens refuse to match the pictures in my field guide and leaves fail to match the foliage key. I can't tell whether the leaf that I hold in my hand is round, oval or elliptical – it seems in between all three. After years of painstaking arboreal study I can now recognise a weeping willow, a monkey puzzle and a Scots pine, and in autumn I can even recognise a horse chestnut and a rowan. As for the rest, they remain for the most part a continuing mystery to me.

As often as not the presence of trees on the hill, especially regimented ranks of exotic conifers, is a nuisance. They bar the way, their branches decapitate the unwary and their roots entangle weary feet. Yet I'm not oblivious to their charms. I like the colours in which they dress autumn, the way their branches wave in the wind and the way they weather the storms and survive in hostile environments against all odds. I also find their size and longevity comforting – a reminder of the continuing saga of life on this planet. But in all my travels there have been only two specimens that have made a lasting impression on me, and coincidentally they supply the answers to two trivia questions.

Question 1: What is the largest living thing on earth? Answer General Sherman, a massive sequoia with an estimated volume of 1486.6 cubic meters that grows at almost 7,000ft on the western slopes of the High Sierra of California. There may be other claimants to the title (in 1992 an underground fungus covering 38 acres was discovered), but none present such an impressive sight as General Sherman and his companions in the cathedral-like Giant Forest.

Question 2: What is the oldest living thing on earth? Answer: Old Methuselah, a bristlecone pine that grows at almost 10,000ft in the White Mountains of California; in 1991 its age was estimated as 4,720. Again there are other claimants to the title, including some creosote plants and lichen whose age may be greater than 10,000 years, but none are as impressive as Old Methuselah. While the sequoias impress by their sheer bulk the bristlecones amaze by their very existence. Their strategy for survival in a desolate landscape is to maintain a thin vein of life in some branches while allowing others to die. They cling obstinately to the parched mountainsides, their bleached, contorted limbs reaching forlornly into the cobalt blue sky, forming shapes that are both grotesque and beautiful at the same time. I have a lot of time for bristlecones.

My general ignorance about flora extends to much of the fauna that crosses my path. When it comes to birds, for instance, I can barely distinguish a sparrow from a stork. Ironically the school prize I won for collecting the most wild flowers was a book on bird spotting. It was the first volume of a set I never completed. Book One – Divers to Hawks; even now it means nothing to me – I still can't tell a cormorant from a shag.

It is unfashionable to say this, and I know some of you may be ardent ornithologists (and I do envy birds their flight capability), but close up they are ugly brutes who have developed little in grace or beauty since the days of the dinosaurs. Moreover, they don't seem to like me either. During my wanderings on the Isle of Skye I was once terrorised by a seagull while beachcombing beneath a sea-cliff during the breeding season. It was like a scene from Hitchcock's *The Birds*. Without warning I was attacked by a seagull that had the size and ferocity of a pterodactyl. Screeching maniacally as it dived out of the sun, it extended its claws and reached for my head. I saw it just in time to duck. It swooped past, banked and came at me from a different angle. I shielded my head with my arm and stumbled on slippery boulders. Again and again this Seagull from Hell came at me before it allowed me to scamper to safety.

The only species of bird for which I have developed any fondness are the oystercatcher and the ptarmigan (sorry to get technical here). The oystercatcher has piped me along many springtime riverside approaches to the hills, and the ptarmigan I love for its shock value. No matter how many times it flies squawking out of the heather it always gives me a start, and when it hobbles away from its nest pretending to have a broken wing, I feel I just have to pursue it so that it doesn't abandon the ruse when a real predator comes along.

I wish I could tell you that in all my escapades in the Scottish Highlands I have seen an eagle, and maybe I have, but maybe it was a buzzard, and once, so a twitcher friend told me, it was a lowly hooded crow. But why an eagle should generate more ornithological excitement than a hoodie is beyond me. Rarity seems a poor criterion on which to make a value judgment, so here's to the unsung silent majority of crows, not one of which family has ever treated me with anything less than diffident friendliness.

Other beasts of the air I have an all too intimate acquaintance with. We're talking mosquitoes, gnats, ticks, no-see-ums, clegs, midges and other forms of flying insect that even to my untrained skin have one thing in common – they bite. More specifically, they go for my blood like a desperate rock climber goes for a jug-handle. There are people who can stand untouched in the middle of a swarm like contestants in a bee-sculpting contest. Not me. As soon as I appear on the scene the word goes out and the sky around me blackens as insect troops muster for the attack. I try to take comfort in the knowledge that it is only the females that bite, and that my increasingly blotched skin is merely proof of my irresistible sexual attraction.

In North America and the northern parts of Europe mosquitoes are the biggest bugbear. Fortunately they are easily spotted and swatted, and protective clothing and potions can keep them at bay, but it is still unnerving to see them hovering in front of your face, sparring for an opening while you try to tuck in to your camp breakfast. Clegs are similarly insistent and inflict the worst bites, but for real horror nothing exceeds being engulfed by a cloud (the correct collective noun is hen-night) of rampant Scottish midges.

Aware of my own susceptibility, I have become an expert on midges and avoid the most infected habitats like a hill-walker avoids ski slopes. The only time I find myself at their mercy is when I'm pitching a tent. Even at the height of summer I undertake this task wearing a biteproof jacket, gloves and balaclava. The only skin remaining to the winged furies is around my eyes, and they go for that like moths to a flame. Soon, in my increasingly frenzied efforts to dodge them, I am doing the dance that has a thousand different names around the world. At Sligachan on the Isle of Skye they call it the Sligachan Square Dance. At Flamingo in the Florida Everglades they call it the Flamingo Foxtrot. From a distance it must indeed seem like I am cavorting dementedly to some unheard tune, but the only discernible musical accompaniment is the rhythmic, almost percussive cursing that distinguishes this dance from all others.

Most of my encounters with animals have been similarly unbeneficial. In Scotland my tent has been ransacked by both mice and hens, in the Alps it was a marmot that nibbled through extra strength cordura to get inside my rucksack, in Corsica I was beset by feral pigs and in Yosemite it was rabid raccoons that sent me scuttling to safety. In both Britain and America, at all altitudes between 0 and 10,000 I have been awakened with a start by those unknown creatures of the night that trip over guy ropes and scamper away to hide silently in wait while you cry out with fright into the darkness.

My most terrifying night experience occurred in the Pyrenees while camped on a wide grassy plain in the mountains. It was the vibrating ground that woke us up. Then we heard neighing and a sound like a stampede – wild horses on the run. Being unfamiliar with the habits of wild horses, yet pretty sure that they did not possess the nocturnal visual capabilities of bats, I had visions of us being trampled to death. There seemed no advantage to be gained by quitting the tent, however, and in any case we were rooted to the spot by fear as the herd galloped ever nearer. And then they were upon us, screeching to a halt at the last moment and snorting monstrously around the hem of the flysheet. The sound was magnified. We dared hardly breathe. And then they were off again as quickly as they had arrived, but we slept not a wink that night.

Even deer, supposedly most gentle of animals, have caused me nothing but trouble. There was that time on An Teallach when a young deer adopted us as foster parents. When we left and drove away it raced alongside through the fields, jumping every hedge in its way in an effort to stay with us. I had to drive at 6omph to dislodge it. Ahh, I hear you say, but what would you have had me do? You are not even safe from them in a minibus, as we found out one winter's night when one prospective Monarch of the Glen stood unconcerned in the middle of the road while our driver slammed on the brakes and skidded into it. We came to a shuddering halt. The deer gave us a look I can only describe as haughty, and in its own good time it ambled away with a headlamp affixed to its rear end.

On another occasion that has since become known as The Attack of the Killer Deer, a deer wrote off my car, an incident about which I had some difficulty convincing the insurance company. As I was driving unconcernedly along Glen Shee this particular monster leapt off the hillside, hit me broadside and ran off to lie in wait for the next unsuspecting motorist. The car was slammed into a ditch; I was unhurt but the car body had been dislodged from its chassis. I now drive more carefully when deer are around.

Although there is one recorded case of a deer killing a

man, and despite the existence of adders and occasional reports of sightings of large cat-like beasts, we are lucky in Britain to have no really dangerous fauna on our hills. It could be worse – there could be bears. I may be tempting fate by saying this, but in all my trips through Rocky Mountain bear country I have never yet seen a bear, neither the black variety (the kind that climbs a tree to get at you) nor the grizzly variety (the kind that simply shakes you out of the tree). I put this down to my superior bear-avoidance skills.

Knowing that bears can do nasty things to a person, I have become an expert on bear lore. I know how to read bear scat, bear-bag food and roll into a foetal position and play dead if charged. I have a bear-bell to warn the beasts of my approach, I avoid groves of succulent berries, I do not camp beside trails, I cook at least one hundred yards from my tent and I carry unperfumed soap and toothpaste. If, despite these preventative measures, I should round a blind corner of the trail and surprise a bear so distracted in some private act that he has not heard my approach, I have contingency plans. I shall not attempt to run away like prey (unless I am with a companion whom I can outrun), I shall not challenge my adversary by looking him in the eye and I shall stand my ground if he charges, knowing that most bear charges are show. As a last resort I also know that people have survived maulings even after having great chunks taken out of them. So why worry?

Armed with such knowledge I have tramped the trails of the Rockies on several occasions unhampered by ursine attentions. There was just one thing missing when I returned from these trips, one thing that would have made the perfect climax to the slide show that I inflict on my family and friends – a photograph of a bear.

My attitude towards bears perhaps sums up my attitude

towards animals in general. I have nothing against them. They have a perfect right to inhabit this planet along with the rest of us. Someone once asked Robert Louis Stevenson if he liked writing. No, he replied, but he liked having written. I feel the same way about animals. I have no great desire to see them, but sometimes it would be nice to *have seen* them.

CHAPTER 12

Scrambling

YOU TAKE A DEEP BREATH and step up. Beneath your feet the ground seems a million miles away. You grip the rock a little more tightly. Beyond your reach a blank, holdless wall curves upwards out of sight. Shifting balance from foot to foot, you cling on with one hand while the other searches for the route onwards. Out of the blankness another hold materialises. Your fingers curl gratefully around it. Your heart beats a little faster. You take a deep breath and step up.

Keeping three points of contact you move one limb at a time, gradually but irresistibly working your way skyward. As you gain height movement becomes less tentative, more composed. Your fingers flit sensuously over the rock, exploring its shape and texture. You are in intimate contact with the mountain. A rush of exhilaration pulses through your body. You beam to revel in the rhythm of the climb. Everyday worries fade away into insignificance. Sky, valley floor and surrounding mountains blend in peripheral vision into a blurred backdrop; at centre stage there exists only the next move, which becomes the focal point of your life.

And then you are at the top. You've made it. Your body glows with satisfaction and you want more of the same. Instead of the easiest lines of ascent you begin to seek out routes that involve putting hand to rock. You want a little more than hands-in-pockets walk-ups. You have become a scrambler.

There is a qualitative difference between scrambling and hillwalking which is more than the fact that one requires the use of the hands while the other does not. It's something to do with the intrinsic nature of the activity; after all, why were we given an opposable thumb if it wasn't to grip rock with? It also has something to do with the nature of rock itself, otherwise we would obtain the same sort of satisfaction from crawling on all fours up steep hillsides, grabbing clumps of grass for purchase, or hauling ourselves from tree root to tree root up wooded precipices.

Of course, not everyone harbours ambitions to scramble, and if you want to keep your hands free for other things then as long as no non-consenting adults, children or animals are involved, it's a free country. But the line of least resistance is not always the best, no matter what your criteria of best. While by definition hills cannot be horizontal they can and do tend to the vertical, and this tendency often produces their most attractive features.

You can stroll up Helvellyn from north or south on a path a mile wide, but if you really want to see the mountain as it was meant to be seen, make the round of the corrie skyline above Red Tarn, scrambling up Swirral Edge and down Striding Edge. (Of course the mountain was meant to be seen in this way, otherwise what would be the point of the corrie?) You can reach the summit of Snowdon by train, but if you really want to see why it attracts such devotion among hillwalkers Welsh and far, balance your way around the Snowdon Horseshoe, starting out along the sharp pinnacled ridge of Crib Goch and finishing above the dark slabs of Y Lliwedd. You can reach the two Munros that support the intervening Aonach Eagach (Notched Ridge) in Glen Coe by easy walks from the glen, but to avoid the ridge itself is to miss a supreme mountaineering experience that is within the capability of most hillwalkers.

Not all British mountains offer the same choice of routes, and if you want to reach certain summits in Scotland you're just going to have to grab some rock. Reaching the central peak of The Cobbler, for instance, involves a crawl through a hole in the rock onto an exposed ledge, followed by a couple of airy step-ups. The less confident may find this manoeuvre facilitated by judicious use of the knees. The summit of Stac Pollaidh is guarded by a rock tower that yields easily once the appropriate jug-handle has been discovered, but the exposure and the prospect of having to reverse the move on descent dissuade many. Measured as a percentage of visitor numbers, perhaps more expletives are uttered here than at any other spot in the Highlands.

On the Hebridean islands things become even more problematical. The traverse of A' Chir on the island of Arran involves the negotiation of an exposed 15ft wall. Of the 11 Munros in the Cuillin of Skye only two (Bruach na Frithe and Sgurr na Ban-achdich) can be climbed without putting hand to rock and then only by one route each. This really is a scrambler's paradise, where the peaks are pointed, the connecting ridges are sharp, the rock is spectacularly rough and the surrounding sea imparts an air of other-worldliness to the whole proceedings.

There is even one Cuillin summit (the only one in the British Isles) that cannot be reached without rock climbing – the infamous inaccessible Pinnacle, which prevents some people from completing their round of the Munros. The drops on each side of this vertiginous blade of rock are so abysmal that the mere sight of them may cause the nervous to sit down and grab the nearest piece of solid ground. The easiest ascents are the Difficult 60ft west ridge and the easier but still Moderate

150ft east ridge. This latter route appears in some scramblers' guidebooks, but there's no way you'd get me on it without a rope and a blindfold. A friend of mine once climbed it and reversed it unroped; he told me he returned shaking.

The distinction between hillwalking and scrambling is easy to define – if you're not using your hands then you're not scrambling. But what is a scramble to me may not be a scramble to you – I've had people stroll nonchalantly past me on slabs where I'm gripping the rock with every point of contact I can muster and losing weight through nervous tension. Establishing the upper limit at which scrambling becomes rock climbing is even more subjective. I've seen the west ridge of the In Pin climbed unroped (although I hardly dared to watch), while at the other extreme I've witnessed a charity roped horizontal climb of a city high street, using lamp posts for belays.

My own definition of the distinction between scrambling and rock climbing is that if it's scary enough to need a rope then it's beyond scrambling. Some scramblers' guidebooks include what they refer to as roped scrambles, but as someone who makes a virtue out of cowardice and is quite prepared to defend this as a moral philosophical position, I am perfectly happy to leave this sort of stuff to others.

Yet something does keep drawing me back to the rock. Perhaps it is a desire to experience more intimate contact with the rock than that afforded by the soles of boots, perhaps it is a desire to explore naked mountain terrain devoid of all vegetation, or perhaps I just need the adrenalin rush. Whatever the reason, there are many times I have set off up the hill intent on some easy grassy summit, only to find myself hours later pinned wonderingly to some insignificant off-route crag.

Those who really get the scrambling bug will eventually fetch up on the continent, where there are enough scrambling

opportunities to last a lifetime and the Dolomites in particular are a scrambler's paradise. Here many routes that would otherwise be the preserve of rock climbers have been made passable to hillwalkers by the construction of *via ferrata* (literally iron roads). Metal ladders, chains and ropes bedeck great walls and ridges and make their passage completely safe, no matter how difficult the move or how vast the void between your legs.

Scrambling on *via ferrata* differs from roped scrambling in that the hardware is attached to the rock not to the scrambler; it is not there to help you climb the route, it is the route itself. Leading or even seconding on a rope may not always inspire the necessary confidence to attempt an exposed move, but clip yourself on to the rung of a ladder using a karabiner attached to a waist loop, and it is amazing what you will try. In my time I have dangled unmoved over enormous drops, climbed ladders hundreds of feet high and swung on ropes around the lips of thundering waterfalls; hard to believe.

Take the Paterkoffel *via ferrata* near Canazei. It tunnels upwards through the rock itself, emerges into open air for an exposed ascent made safe by wire ropes and finishes up a steep wall on thin ledges. The route is so popular that on the final section, at least a Difficult rock climb without the fixed wire as a lifeline, it is often necessary for scramblers to clamber over each other as they go up and down. But so engrossing are the technicalities of krab management that this becomes amusing rather than terrifying.

If you're into scrambling, then the *via ferrata* can become addictive, so it is a pity there is none in Britain. Why not fix a chain handrail on the pinnacled sections of Aonach Eagach? Vandalism! Why not fix ropes on the In Pin or Curved Ridge, that spectacular Moderate route up Buachaille Etive Mor?

Sacrilege! Why not fix ladders on a single route on the north face of Ben Nevis, to make close-up views of Britain's greatest cliff face available to all? Desecration!

But why should rock climbers have it all to themselves? Surely there is room for an occasional *via ferrata*. After all, no-one objects to the short section of chain that aids progress on the West Highland Way along the craggy shores of Loch Lomond or the pegged crag on one of the stalkers' paths up Sgurr a' Mhaoraich. Even Yosemite Valley in California, perhaps the world's most spectacular mountain enclave, has room for one *via ferrata* that puts the summit of spectacular Half Dome within the reach of most. I count my ascent of Half Dome as one of the most memorable days I have spent on the hill and give thanks to those engineers who made it possible.

From any angle in Yosemite, Half Dome is some mountain. Its sheer granite faces look impossibly vertical, as though even Spider-man would need to be on good form to find a route up them. Yet dozens of hillwalkers make the ascent every day in summer thanks to the *via ferrata* up the mountain's north-east face. This incredible piece of engineering takes the form of a cableway consisting of two wire handrails, fixed to pairs of iron posts drilled into the rock at intervals of about 20ft, with wooden crossboards between the posts to provide resting places. 900ft of cableway over a vertical distance of 400ft at an angle of 45 degrees. From below it looks terrifying; it even surmounts small overhangs, for goodness sake.

The adrenalin is really pumping as we start up. We haul ourselves hand over hand from crossboard to crossboard, forcing ourselves to lean backwards to get the whole soles of our boots onto the rock to maximise friction. Don't look down! As the exposure increases so does my nervousness and I grip the handrails ever more tightly. There is absolutely no reason to fall, I tell myself. At the overhangs I hit my chin with my knee. My arms ache but that's a minor concern. Don't look down! Twenty minutes later we arrive at the plateau summit, our throats parched in the afternoon heat from having forgotten to close our mouths.

Flushed with success I stand gingerly on the Diving Board, a projection of rock that hangs over Yosemite Valley 5,000ft below. We put off the descent, knowing that it will force us to face the void beneath our feet, but we cannot wait forever. We pluck up courage and go for it. The cableway disappears over the edge in intimidating fashion. The angle is easy at first and I face forward, pulling up on the swaying handrails to keep them taut and leaning forward to keep my legs at right angles to the rock. But I soon realise that as the angle increases I shall be leaning out over the abyss, so I carefully turn around and descend backwards. Sliding my hands down the wires, I lower myself from one crossboard to the next, feeling with my foot as the handrails lead down over an overhang. Remember to breathe, I keep telling myself.

And then we're down. We have suffered small finger burns and wish we had used the old gloves from the pile provided, but we've made it. We join others who sit in silence and stare at the hair-raising route above our heads, unable to take our eyes away. The vast granite wall sparkles in the afternoon sun. The following evening we stand on Glacier Point and watch the setting sun paint a red wash over the summit of Half Dome. Yosemite Valley is in darkness far below and the snowy High Sierra crest is dimly visible as a dusky backdrop. I turn to my companion. It may just be the setting sun but her face is aglow.

CHAPTER 13

Accidents

YOU WOULDN'T THINK HILLWALKERS would want to dwell on their accidents. You'd think maybe they'd be squeamish about blood and broken limbs. Not a bit of it. You wouldn't think they'd want to brag about their lack of foresight or hillcraft. You'd think they'd shrink from reliving the moment. No way. Unlike bungee jumpers, cavers, cyclists, car drivers and almost anyone else who leaves his armchair to venture into the risky world outside, they seem to revel in the finer details of accidents and find joy in any injury this side of permanent. The longer the fall, the more excruciating the pain, the greater the spillage of blood, the more salivatingly relished the tale. Some even sing about it, for goodness sake, as witnessed by the following out-pouring of sympathy:

He Ain't Gonna Climb No More

They scraped him off the corrie like a pound of raspberry jam,
They scraped him off the corrie like a pound of raspberry jam,
They scraped him off the corrie like a pound of raspberry jam,
And he ain't gonna climb no more.

Chorus:

Glory, glory, what a helluva way to die,
Glory, glory, what a helluva way to die,
Glory, glory, what a helluva way to die,
And he ain't gonna climb no more.

They packed him in a rucksack and they sent him home to Mum.
They telescoped his vertebrae into a sardine tin.
I'd like to meet the second who put the belay on.
I'd like to meet the author of this bloody awful guide.

What is this fascination with accidents? Does singing about them lessen their fearfulness? Is surviving a longer fall than your neighbour some kind of one-upmanship? Is breaking a leg supposed to give you superior hill cred? Is an accident some kind of bizarre hillcraft initiation ceremony? When we regale our colleagues with our tales of terror, are we seeking their sympathy, rejoicing in our survival or merely flaunting our ability to thumb our noses at adversity?

In the course of my adventures on the hill I have had cause to ask myself such questions on several occasions, and whenever I begin to examine my experiences and feelings I am always drawn back to the Cuillin, which is always a good place to spill a little blood. The sharp rock, famously referred to in an old guidebook as 'painfully adhesive', removes fingerprints and shreds skin at the best of times, and it doesn't take much effort to drum up an accident.

My first and so far bloodiest injury on the Cuillin occurred when I slipped and cracked my shin on a sharp boulder. By the time I got back to Glen Brittle campsite I was in considerable pain, and when I rolled up the leg of my breeches I found my sock welded to my skin by caked blood. It was an impressive sight even to hardened Glen Brittle crag rats, and a crowd soon gathered to offer advice. Amputation was widely advocated and someone produced a stick to put between my teeth in case I needed to be held down. Only after repeated reassurances did I allow someone to soak my leg in water, whereupon the sock freed itself and the wound beneath turned out to be so disappointingly trivial that my circle of new-found friends immediately drifted back to their tents again. So much for my fifteen minutes of celebrity.

More serious for the wounded, but equally enjoyable for spectators and doctors, was a series of accidents in which my colleagues and I were involved while learning to rock climb on a local crag. It began with a bruised shin whose owner we deposited at the the local hospital for a check-up. A broken wrist and a cracked rib, together with assorted cuts and abrasions, soon followed. We injured ourselves climbing up that crag, climbing down it, abseiling off it and even standing at the bottom looking up at it, owing to an unstable base surrounded by gorse bushes like pin cushions. There can have been few more pleasing moments in our lives than to see one of our number disappear squealing into the welcoming embrace of those gorse bushes.

In retrospect it occurs to me that perhaps there was something amiss with our rope technique, for like lemmings we fell off that crag every which way you could imagine. One fall stands out in memory as being at the same time both the best and the worst, depending on whether you were called Robin or whether you were merely hanging around watching Robin climb. His attempted ascent turned unexpectedly into a rapid descent in which he ricocheted balletically off a tree and landed in a heap at our feet. The ground broke his fall and also his elbow, part of the bone of which disappeared into the hidden recesses of his arm and was never found.

I often wonder what our friends the doctors at the local hospital made of that one. They became accustomed to our regular visits and we did not like to disappoint them. They may even have unwittingly planted an unconscious desire within us to give them something interesting to work on, and perhaps that explains why John and I fell down a snow slope in Glen Coe. With winter at hand and the rock climbing season long past, perhaps we felt that the doctors would be missing us. Perhaps we needed to relive those heady summer visits to out-patients and provide the medical staff with some amusement until the lemming season opened again.

One advantage that the Glen Coe accident had over our summer escapades was its excessive goriness, which enabled us to dine out on it for weeks, for during our headlong flight down from our high point in a snow gully, John managed to hole his upper lip with his flailing ice axe. I seemed to come out of the fall with nothing more than a twisted knee and was able to drive him back to our hospital, where the doctors were inordinately pleased to see us and grateful that we had gone to all that trouble just for them.

John was duly stitched and bandaged and was soon joking about the accident along with the rest of them. Meanwhile I found myself in increasing pain and the doctors were able to obtain renewed pleasure from our visit by X-raying my knee. And so, by some ironic twist of fate, it came to pass that whereas I drove John to the hospital he had to drive me away, my leg bandaged heavily from hip to ankle. In the weeks to come the doctors X-rayed my knee in positions more surreal than any I have attempted on a rock face, but much to their chagrin the offending limb recovered before they could determine the cause of the problem.

As if to punish me for this effrontery they passed me over to a physiotherapist in whose clutches I experienced more pain than a man was designed to bear. During sessions whose details I am still trying to expunge from memory, this creature of dubious humanity and parentage, who could well have learned his craft from the Spanish Inquisition, would punch and pummel me until I begged for mercy, at which point he would peel me off the ceiling and begin all over again. After that I made sure I never again recovered from injury until my doctors gave me the go-ahead.

I don't mean to impugn the honour of the medical profession, for I remember my doctors' skill and ghoulish humour

with fondness. In my experience only mountain rescue teams have exceeded them in blackness of humour. Perhaps it is an emotional defence mechanism for dealing with tragedy. While walking in the Cairngorms some friends of mine once found a perfectly preserved dead hillwalker in a springtime snowdrift; he had lain where he had died until snowmelt revealed his body and my friends passed by. Unsure of how to handle the situation, they improvised a stretcher out of ice axes and spare clothing and carried the body out to Braemar. Like many who find themselves involved in mountain rescue, they found the situation darkly humorous and later admitted to uncontrollable fits of giggling, like in a scene from a black comedy.

This incident reminds me of another that gave me one of the biggest frights of my life. It occurred while I was exploring a cave in northern Scotland. As I rounded a corner my torch beam caught two hands sticking upright out of the mud, reaching for the air. I recoiled in horror, but on closer inspection discovered nothing more frightening than a pair of rubber gloves, left in that position by some diabolically inspired caver who, in his absence, came in for some concerted and highly detailed abuse.

The two most hilarious accidents in which I have been involved occurred not while hillwalking, in fact not while moving at all, but simply while watching someone else rock climb. They both occurred on the Buachaille Etive Mor, the great rock peak that guards the entrance to Glen Coe. On one occasion I was sitting with a friend at the foot of a chimney while two colleagues climbed above us. Suddenly we heard a shout informing us that part of the mountain had detached itself from the rest and was on its way down. Naturally I grabbed the nearest thing I could lay my hands on, which happened to be my friend's rucksack, and placed it over my head.

My friend also reached for his rucksack, but I was quicker. While his arm was still outstretched a rock landed on his head and he keeled over in slow motion. The image still brings a smile to my face, but he never did see the funny side of it, even after he had recovered.

On the second occasion I was more directly involved as second man on the rope, belaying in a gully beside a face on which my partner led out. When he fell onto a running belay the strain came on my fixed belay, which instantly became unfixed. Before I had time to adopt a dignified position for take-off I found myself sailing across the cliff with a bewildered look on my face, only to meet my dangling and even more bewildered partner on his way back. For some reason I had the presence of mind to hang on to the rope, and from a mid-air stance I lowered my partner to a ledge from where he belayed me while I clambered to safety. Laugh, we could have died!

At least these incidents involved others with whom the experience could be shared and discussed in the bar afterwards. There is nothing more frustrating than being involved in an accident to which there is no witness; it seems to destroy the whole point of the exercise. Like the time I was upended by a lurking riverside boulder and executed a perfect swallow dive into the foaming torrent. I even remembered to roll with the fall to avoid injury on submerged rocks. There was no-one around to appreciate my skill then, nor when I survived a 1,000ft high-speed descent of a twisting snow gully perched atop a small avalanche. I came to a halt in a heap of avalanche debris, hyperventilating; my spectacles sailed past fully five minutes later and I merely had to put out my hand to grab them.

The one time I have been in real difficulty while hillwalking also occurred when alone, on descent from the summit of Columbine Peak, a 12,652ft scramblers' peak in the Sierra Nevada of California. I was unacclimatised and exhausted, and after reaching the summit my concentration deserted me, followed swiftly by my balance. I landed astride a huge wedge of rock so damaging my pelvis, shin and ankle that I did not have enough hands to clutch everything that was throbbing. This was serious – I could tell by the way I was writhing around. I consoled myself with the fact that I could still father children.

I recovered sufficiently to stagger back to my backcountry campsite two days walking distance from the nearest road-head. Not that the distance mattered, because by the following morning my swollen ankle would no longer fit into my boot. Still, I was camped in a fine spot and I could use the time to acclimatise. Did I survive, you ask? Yes, I did, and I now look back on that time as a supreme test of my survival skills and tell the tale in bars along with the rest of them. Do you want to see my scars?

One day, if fate so decrees, perhaps I shall die on the hill. I am reminded of a wonderfully fatalistic drawing by the French artist Samivel, in which the route taken by an ascending climber and a falling rock intersect at the same point in time; it is called *The Rendezvous*. If my hillwalking career should end in such a way then at least I shall have the satisfaction of knowing that I did not grow old gracefully. And if not, then scatter my ashes on some mountainside and let them blow to the winds. Perhaps some of my friends will visit the spot for a while, perhaps I shall be remembered for a generation or so, then I shall be lost to history. No matter. In the words of Christina Rossetti, 'Better by far you should forget and smile than you should remember and be sad'. Meanwhile, when I survive an accident it gives me satisfaction to know that the grim reaper hasn't claimed me yet. That at least is something to be joyful about.

CHAPTER 14

Epics

I LOVE A GOOD EPIC. You can keep your roadside rambles, seashore strolls, wayside wanderings and moorland meanderings. Give me a good epic any day. Now don't get me wrong, I'm not proposing anything that Safetyman need worry about. I'm not suggesting you take to the hill in a blizzard for a character-forming battle against the elements, and return to earth in the wee small hours with helicopters whirling around overhead, but... let me give you some examples.

It came to pass one wintry November morn that I found myself in Glen Nevis surrounded by snow-capped peaks. I had never done any serious winter hillwalking before, but an ice axe was thrust into my hand and I was ushered onto the hill by the leader of our party, an Alpinist of some years experience. After practising how to hold an axe, how to brake with it and, more importantly from our leader's point of view, how not to stab him with it when we were anywhere within flailing distance, we followed him up into the abode of the snow, obediently dogging his every bootprint.

As I later discovered, we were attempting the Ring of Steall, a nine-mile loop around the great corrie at the head of Glen Nevis from which issues 300ft Steall waterfall. Once onto the skyline we followed our intrepid leader uncomplainingly across the narrow Devil's Ridge, blissfully unaware of the exposure and revelling in our new-found winter mountaineering ability. Other tops followed in quick succession but not quickly enough as the short November day drew to a close. As darkness approached there still seemed an awfully long way to go, but similar situations must have occurred in the Alps and presumably our leader knew what he was doing, so stepped we gaily on we went.

Finally, when it was becoming difficult to see and yet another peak loomed before us, our leader turned to us, informed us that it would be prudent to leave it for another day and head down into the corrie and, by the way, could we get out our torches? Torches? We looked at each other nonplussed. Nobody had told us to bring torches. How were we supposed to know that it got dark in the Highlands?

And thus our party of six began a slow, stumbling descent with the aid of our leader's one torch, which thank goodness he had had the foresight to bring. Even moonlight could do little to speed our progress, and when our leader began to mutter darkly we felt that we had let him down. It was then that we began to hear the roaring. It grew louder as we walked. Our leader looked puzzled, or perhaps it was a trick of the moonlight. When the noise became deafening we edged forward on hands and knees and found ourselves peering over the lip of Steall waterfall. Water billowed out over the abyss.

Our leader swore. We had descended into the wrong corrie. Obviously this winter hillwalking game was going to be more difficult than I had anticipated. Without a word he opened his rucksack and pulled out a rope. What forethought! How lucky we were to have such a leader. But when he asked who was going to be the first to abseil, the bewildered look returned to our faces. We looked at each other as though he were speaking a foreign language, which of course he was – abseil? I will say this for him – he took the news calmly. He did no more than sigh, belay, tie one of my unsuspecting companions on to the end of the rope and drop her over the edge.

Just like that. One second she was there, the next second she wasn't. Where had she gone? The rope would surely not reach the foot of the 300ft waterfall? What trick did our leader have now to extricate us from this new predicament? I soon found out. I was next to go. Ignoring my whimpered protestations, he tied me to the rope and ushered me to the lip of the waterfall. Aim for that ledge, he said, pointing vaguely down towards the glen. Obviously I wasn't experienced enough to have eyesight as good as his. All I could see was wet vertical slabs disappearing into the blackness.

In a voice that brooked no argument he ordered me to the edge, where I knelt down, turned around and felt for a foothold. I think it was about this point that I lost what little nerve I had left. My grip followed shortly afterwards and I found myself swinging haplessly across Steall waterfall. I suppose I could have viewed the occasion as a wonderful opportunity to study the upper topography of one of Britain's most spectacular cascades in greater detail than had previously been vouchsafed to a man. Instead I just yelled.

The next thing I remember was landing wet and crumpled on a grassy ledge some 100ft down. A figure lurched at me out of the darkness. It was my predecessor on this journey into the unknown. She untied me from the rope and it whooshed back up the cliff out of sight. At irregular intervals thereafter the remainder of our party dropped out of the sky and displaced us further along the ledge. It became quite cosy, but we talked little and saw even less until our leader abseiled onto us with his torch. Below us lay a steep slabby hillside that with care we were informed we could negotiate by swinging Tarzan-like from tree to tree. And that we did, and later – much, much later – we reminisced about the expert mountaincraft of our leader and our wonderful day on the hill.

So ended an episode that seems to me to have all the elements required of an epic. Firstly it was unplanned; by definition an epic must be unexpected. If you go for a twenty-mile hillwalk at 9pm and don't return until the following morning then I'm sorry, it doesn't count. Secondly, it was long. It is impossible to have an epic, no matter how unexpected, if the whole episode lasts a mere ten minutes. Thirdly, it involved an above-average degree of difficulty for those involved. When I came to know our leader better I realised that for him the Ring of Steall episode was well within the bounds of normality, but for the rest of us it was an experience which, no matter how much we joked about it in public, I suspect we each privately would not have wished to repeat.

What constitutes a 'good' epic is something else again. In the best epics no-one is hurt; you may return with the odd scar to display to admiring acolytes, but you sustain no injury you would not want. And companions with whom to share the experience are useful, otherwise no-one may believe you. Yet surely there must be something more.... Here is a bad epic to help me pin down exactly what I'm trying to say.

My very first experience of snow was also my very first experience (and nearly my last) of hillwalking: a school expedition to Snowdon in February, led by Teacher. I was fourteen years old. On our very first day we attempted Snowdon by the path from Llanberis. As this follows a railway track all the way to the summit, presumably Teacher thought no difficulties would be encountered. He was wrong. The train doesn't stop running in winter for no reason, it stops because the railway cutting disappears beneath a uniform, convex bank of snow that plummets into the deep basin of Cwm Clogwyn.

Our party of about a dozen schoolchildren reached the snowline at three quarter way station without difficulty, and here we stopped for lunch. Teacher decided he had had enough at this point because his boots were slipping on the increasingly icy path, but those of us who wished to continue could do so as the summit was not far distant. Three of us took up the challenge and headed up into the cloud. The cutting soon disappeared under snow, to be replaced by a narrow path along what remained of its outer edge, beaten out by previous walkers. The snowbank on the uphill side of the path was hard and icy, on the downhill side nothing could be seen except swirling mist. The wind increased alarmingly, causing white-out conditions and ripping my flimsy nylon overtrousers.

It dawned on us, for all our young bravado, that we were out of our depth. We sat down, huddled together and waited for something, we didn't know what, to happen. When nothing did happen we decided to retreat, and that's when we discovered that it's easier to ascend than descend hard snow. All the footprints seemed to be sloping away from us, towards the edge. And then one of my companions slipped.

If you have ever stood helplessly by and watched someone slide uncontrollably down a snow slope, grasping for non-existent handholds, you will know that it seems to happen in slow motion, as if you are watching a movie at the wrong speed. Worse still, you are a mere spectator and there is nothing you can do about it. I watched my friend slide off the path and over the edge. It seemed as though there was nothing that could save him but miraculously, when all seemed lost, the toe of one boot clung on to some smear of rock that protruded through the snow, and he hung there, swaying gracefully.

Still we, his companions, remained rooted to the spot as we watched him flail at the snow with his hands until he regained some semblance of safety. The incident scared the wits out of all of us. We continued our descent on feet, hands and as many other points of bodily contact with the ground as we could find. My shredded overtrousers billowed out horizontally from my waist and I was thoroughly distressed.

To add insult to injury, when we reached the rest of the party at three-quarter way station, we were greeted not with concern and relief but with a reprimand for keeping them waiting. As we descended to Llanberis I lagged further and further behind, still clutching at my useless overtrousers, suffering from what in retrospect I now know was incipient exposure. I followed the party mechanically at a distance. No-one seemed to care whether I made it or not. Perhaps what distinguishes good epics like the Ring of Steall from bad epics such as this is an absence of fear and suffering.

You would think such an introduction to hillwalking would have put me off for life, but during that week in Wales I reached the top of two mountains and when I returned home to confront the narrowness of family life I took to my room and cried.

Another day, another epic. The Lairig Ghru – the 28-mile pass through the heart of the Cairngorms from Braemar to Aviemore. Winter. Beneath an overcast sky and in an increasingly strong wind, Judith and I completed the first half of the journey and camped near Corrour Bothy, that remote and unpretentious shelter in the heart of the pass. The following morning we set off in high spirits for the summit of the pass and the fleshpots of Aviemore, but it soon became obvious that we weren't going to make it. Wind and swirling snow combined to produce a phenomenon known in that part of the country as a blind-drift, and near the summit of the pass we kept blundering into windblown walls of snow that completely blocked the route. We were forced back to Corrour bowed and exhausted.

We tried to pitch the tent again, but the wind ripped the flysheet apart and we had no choice but to seek shelter in the bothy with other stranded walkers. We slept not at all, but the following morning our spirits soared as we rose to greet a beautiful day of blue sky, sun and crisp snow crunching satisfyingly underfoot. With renewed energy and enthusiasm we crossed the pass, completed our journey to Aviemore and concurred that all was well with the world.

Only once have I enjoyed an epic more, and that was one that had everything you could possibly wish for – unexpectedness, difficulty, length and enough thrills to last for many a day. It began with a long walk-in from Strath Croe in Kintail to Alltbeithe youth hostel, situated at the remote head of Glen Affric. From here Wendy and I took a stalkers' path up into the clouds that swirled around Sgurr nan Ceathreamhnan, and reached the summit via a knife-edge ridge of snow where gusts of sleet battered us backwards in our steps. Nothing unusual so far.

As with many epics, it was only on descent that things began to get out of hand. The wind increased (always a good sign) and the mother of all downpours hit us as we descended below cloud level. Still there seemed nothing to write home about until the hillside steepened and we found ourselves negotiating flumes of long wet grass. All it took was one fateful step onto one particularly slippery blade and I was airborne. On splashdown gravity took me under its wing and I picked up speed as I hurtled glenwards. Only a mud-spattered shelf of level ground saved my hillwalking career from an unseemly end by grabbing my flailing body and holding it in its sticky grip until I skidded to a halt.

I was bruised and battered but no more. The greatest insult was to my dignity as leader of the party, and so I shrugged off the incident as though it had been good fun. Less effort than walking, I told Wendy as I limped ahead. The rain was incredible. Every minor stream over which we had stepped on the outward journey was now a foaming torrent that had to be forded with care. And there were a thousand more of these streams than previously.

Darkness fell (another good sign for epic seekers), but I

was now more experienced than I had been on Steall waterfall and we had head torches with which to continue the long day's journey into night. Nevertheless, the rain was so thick that it reflected and dispersed the light from the torch beams, reducing visibility to a few yards.

The route back to Strath Croe led across the flat plain at the head of Loch a' Bhealaich, where deep, slowly moving streams overflowed their banks and became indistinguishable from the dark moorland. We developed a strategy. Using our ice axes as sounding devices, we were able to detect rivers before we fell into them. This enabled us to slowly lower ourselves into the water until our feet touched bottom and wade across to the far bank hand in hand, moving one at a time for safety. After we had negotiated the plain in this way the path took to drier ground as it climbed over a pass, but we knew that the route still had one sting in its tail – the Allt Coire an Sgairne. This is the river that carries most of the drainage on the north side of Ben Fhada, which is not called the Long Mountain in Gaelic for nothing.

The river appeared in our torch beams like a seething whirlpool. I stood on the near bank and watched the turbulent white water rush past, but I knew that if I contemplated its power for too long I would shrink from doing what had to be done. With a deep breath I lowered myself thigh deep into the icy maelstrom, but I dared not let go of the bank and Wendy had to pull me out again. I searched up and down the seemingly impassable barrier but no weakness appeared. Wendy looked resigned to her fate; either the leader would find a way out or he would not, why worry about it?

The only possible route across seemed to centre on an underwater boulder ruckle that was currently acting as the lip of a small waterfall. If the pool below was not too deep and the boulders had good handholds... I launched myself into the torrent once more, dived for the first boulder and embraced it like a long-lost lover. Water swept over my head and down my neck; I hardly noticed it. I swung to the next boulder, tacking against the force of the river. Wendy dived in beside me. Using an arm jam I helped her across to my boulder, she helped me to the next... We were across.

In the days to come, when Wendy told of our exploits, friends commiserated with her. On occasion she still admonishes me for the times I have put her through. But I swear there is a gleam in her eye. You can keep your roadside rambles, seashore strolls, wayside wanderings and moorland meanderings. Give me a good epic any day.

CHAPTER 15

Wilderness and Backpacking

LIKE ERIC SHIPTON I HAVE always been intoxicated by the idea of wilderness. A glimpse of a map showing vast expanses of roadless country can cure me of any depression, and if that country contains mountains then as far as I'm concerned it's the promised land.

Most of the time the wilderness is out of bounds to me; I can only nibble at its perimeter in one – or two-day bites. The chance to feast on the succulent interior comes but once or twice a year in the form of holidays, and I anticipate those precious meals like a starving glutton. How some people can spend their holidays on the Costa del Shell-suit surrounded by a rush of humanity is beyond my comprehension.

Cultural holidays also leave me cold. The Parthenon may be a magnificent edifice, the Colosseum may have rich historical significance, the Flemish masters may have painted fine works of art, but if I had to spend my holidays in Athens, Rome or Amsterdam I would die from terminal frustration. I need my fix of wild places. After two weeks in the Jotunheimen maybe I won't mind taking a tour of Oslo, at the end of the John Muir Trail maybe I'll be content to take in the sights of San Francisco and when I come down from the Pyrenees maybe, just maybe, you'll get me to sit on a Mediterranean beach for a few moments. But don't bet on it.

What is this wilderness I crave? My dictionary tells me it is 'wild, uninhabited and uncultivated land', in which case there are city gardens that would qualify. Surely size is also important: wilderness has to take time to get out of. Outside its perimeter lie civilisation, safety, sustenance, shelter and aid. The unavailability of and lack of easy access to these is for me a necessary condition of the wilderness experience.

To some extent, then, wilderness is a state of mind. Some may be able to find it a few hours walk away from the road-side. For many more it has to take at least a day or two to get out of, and unfortunately this makes Britain severely deficient in it, for there are very few places on this island where you can walk in a straight line for a day without reaching a road. I have personally experienced wilderness in the Norwegian Jotunheimen, the Spanish Pyrenees and the American West, but this only reflects my own state of mind. Some hikers who learn their hillcraft in the Rockies have to disappear into the Alaskan backcountry to find their wilderness.

It is of course possible to find solitude on British hills, even if you have to choose your place and time with great care. Pitch a tent half way up Scafell Pike or Snowdon and climb to the summit by moonlight and you will have even these popu-lar mountains to yourself, while Scotland still has many places where it is possible to escape the madding crowd. Many Corbetts (hills between 2,500ft and 3,000ft high) are only occasionally climbed in these Munro bagging times. The old Thieves' Road, used by the clans of Lochaber in times past to plunder the fertile lands of Moray, still crosses only one paved road in its 100 mile journey across the breadth of the Grampian Mountains. Other long-distance cross-country routes abound. On the Hebridean islands there are still some remote spots that hardly ever see the imprint of a boot.

Ironically, at a time when Britain's and the world's supply of wilderness is diminishing, it could be said that there is more land approaching wilderness status in the Scottish Highlands and Islands today than there has been for many hundreds of years. Certainly it is less inhabited and more appealing to seekers of solitude. Before the Highlands were forcibly cleared of people to make way for sheep farming in the nineteenth century, the glens were highly populated and corries reverberated to the sounds of summer shielings. Bothies and broken walls remain as poignant reminders of those times, and perhaps those of us who love to 'get away from it all' should sometimes pause to reflect on the fact that we owe the emptiness of the Highlands to one of the most tragic episodes in Scottish history.

But the Highlands are hardly wilderness. There are always comparatively easy escape routes to civilisation. Perhaps only the Fisherfield Forest east of Ullapool an area I have come to know as The Last Great Wilderness, can offer a true wilderness experience in Britain. Here, uncrossed by road and virtually untouched by the hand of man, are over 100 square miles of mountain, loch and peat bog. Although minuscule by global standards, if wilderness is in the mind then for me this just about qualifies.

I used to make solo backpacking trips into the heart of this land every Easter to recharge the batteries. Spring is a wonderful time of year there, with snow still capping the peaks and variable weather producing both sun and snow showers, which are funnelled through the glens like express trains. After a couple of days communing with nature I felt refreshed and ready to return to the fray.

Untrammelled land such as the Fisherfield Forest is an increasingly precious commodity in the modern world and is surely worth fighting to preserve. Look at what has happened in Nepal. Twenty years ago my greatest aim in hillwalking was to walk from Katmandu to Everest base camp. At the time it seemed impossible that I could ever fulfill such a fantasy, yet the route is now a crowded, littered thoroughfare beset by tea rooms. And I no longer want to go. It's too late. As improved communications shrink the world my dreams change. Now I look to the west.

Not so long ago North America was a dream to most Brits; now Florida is a top holiday destination and the wilderness of the Rockies, the High Sierra, Alaska and Canada is becoming ever more reachable. Travelling alone for weeks at a time in this uninhabited country, much of which is preserved in law as pristine wilderness and where it can take days of ascent to reach a col at the end of a valley, can really put your life into perspective. There are no easy escape routes here. This is The Big Empty. There is just you and the land, and I shall be ever grateful for what I have discovered in that land.

For those on a tight schedule there are easy ways of getting into the American wilderness. You can ride in on horseback, have your gear packed in while you walk, hire a llama to carry your gear in or get dropped in by plane (in Alaska, where even one third of the inhabitants have no road connection to the rest of the country, flying may be the only practicable way to reach certain areas). If, like me, your budget is usually even tighter than your schedule, the only other way to reach the wilderness is to walk in, preferably in a manner that leaves the land undisturbed by your passage through it.

As a temporary guest in the wilderness, my ideal is to enjoy it without destroying any part of it. This means no fires, no collecting of rocks or flora and no undue disturbance of the land. My aim, as someone who aspires to ecological awareness, is to travel without impact, 'taking only photographs and leaving only footprints.'

If I wish to walk in the wilderness my ethics therefore dictate that I take all my food, heating and shelter with me, and that I carry it all myself on my back. I once saw a photograph in a book about Himalayan exploration of a Hindu ascetic who lived at high altitude and wandered across the snowy wastes with nothing but a loin cloth and a smile, his bare, toughened feet impervious to frostbite. What he lived off is anyone's guess. I could never be like that nor want to be. If nothing else, I like my wilderness comforts too much: a cosy tent, a warm sleeping bag and regular hot meals. I carry all these (and more) in a pack which on a long trip becomes a friend in the wilderness, supplying my every requirement, including even companionship.

There is something inordinately satisfying about back-packing around wild land completely self-sufficient. There is something sublimely liberating about being able to wander and sleep where you will, walking from dawn to dusk if you so wish or stopping a couple of hours after breaking camp, perhaps tempted by a patch of sparkling riverside grass beneath a towering rock peak. Or maybe you choose not to move at all and simply while away the day watching the sun cross the sky.

Of course, it takes a day or two to settle into this mode of existence. At first, my mind still in city mode, I find myself setting targets to be reached. The pack feels heavy; progress is slower than I had expected. But then the magic begins to happen and material civilisation, that *ersatz* impoverished environment to which we have adapted and by doing so alienated ourselves from our origins, fades away like a bad dream. I stop fighting. I succumb to the diurnal rhythms of nature. I begin to feel I belong here. My plans become open-ended. I feel myself regenerating.

How simple and satisfying life is in the wilderness, where even time, which runs my normal day-to-day existence, is irrelevant. In the wilderness I rise at dawn and retire at sunset. I carry a small clock and if dawn feels too early to me I put time forward a couple of hours (to Trail Standard Time) and pretend I am having a lie-in. Making time fit in with my plans in this way, rather than vice-versa, gives me a wonderful feeling of being in control of my life. If only I could retain that feeling when I return to the rat race!

My day in the wilderness begins when the sun hits my tent. Maybe I decide to call that 8am TST. I rise to greet the day and survey my domain. This campsite, this patch of land, this lost fragment of the universe, is my temporary home. It has nothing to interest property developers but to me it is idyllic. A strip of flat green grass, a portable home, running water and views that stop you in your tracks. I like to explore my campsite. I want to know it intimately, to fit it into my cognitive map. I wonder around to view it from all angles, I explore the rocks and flowers, I hunt out the best boulder to sit on and the

best place to extract water from the stream. Gradually I begin to understand this spot and its place in the greater landscape. I begin to feel an affinity with it, until I become assimilated and am no longer an intruder.

The routines of breaking camp in preparation for departure become a therapeutic ritual: rolling up the sleeping bag and mattress, preparing and eating breakfast, washing self and pans at a pollution-proof distance from the stream, dismantling the tent, cramming all the paraphernalia of backpacking into its allotted space in the pack. Finally all that remains to be done is to hoist the pack up onto my back and I am ready to be on my way. Another day in the wilderness awaits.

Who knows what that day will bring? Perhaps a glorious riverside trail lined by alpine flowers. Perhaps a desert of rock and scree, or a pass made laborious by melting snow. Maybe it will be hot or cold, the views breathtaking or non-existent. Everything is contingent and outwith my control, which induces a supremely heady feeling of freedom. Why worry about anything when there is nothing I can do about it? The sheer scale of my surroundings makes me feel at the same time both humble and vital: I feel very unimportant in the vast landscape yet also incredibly powerful, because I have adapted to this country and taken it into my soul.

Adding to this feeling is the knowledge that a simple accident, resulting in a minor injury such as a twisted ankle, can cut my lifeline to civilisation. Some find this prospect overwhelming and frightening, whereas I find it adds to my sense of freedom. It makes me confront the fact that I am mortal, that I am not indispensable after all and that the responsibilities I have taken upon myself back there in the tamed world need not weigh so heavily upon me – the world will get along fine without me. If I have ventured into the wilderness alone these feelings are heightened even more. It is a wonderful feeling to share experiences on the hill with like-minded souls, but there is no getting away from the fact that companions dilute the wilderness experience by their very presence. All of my most deeply moving wilderness experiences have occurred when alone.

I think of how my heart turned over as I sat eating a late meal in the High Sierra and happened to turn around and see Mount Spencer suddenly catch fire, its flanks glowing like hot coals in the setting sun. And the time I stood shivering in the cold night air beneath the overwhelming north face of Stroud Peak in the Wind River Range, its anvil shape hovering over my head, so solid yet so ethereal. And the desolation of Berg Lake in the Canadian Rockies, its milky blue waters suddenly churned up by a crashing block of ice carved from one of Mt. Robson's glaciers. And Matterhorn-shaped Mt. Assini-boine in the Canadian Rockies, whose dawn reflection in the mirror-like surface of serene Lake Magog was solid enough to make the senses reel in confusion. And the fairytale Enchantment Lakes in the Cascade Range of Washington, where lake upon lake fills the hollows between impossible rock peaks to make a jumbled and intimate landscape that is too pretty for words.

I think about how such wilderness experiences have become alien to urban society. About the challenge and exhilaration of travelling across wild land under your own steam. About the planning of the day's trek and the satisfaction of carrying out that plan. About the sorority and fraternity of fellow hikers who cross your path on the trail. About the sheer restfulness of having to concentrate solely on your next foot placement, totally centred in the present. About the peace of exhaustion.

Now, as I sit in my tent with only the roar of the wind for

company, I tell myself that when this trip is over I shall remember how it was and not allow myself to sink back into the stresses and strains of everyday life. I have gained a new perspective on them. I shall keep my mind on the higher ground. Wilderness has taught me this.

Envoi

Titcomb Basin, Wind River Range, Wyoming, USA.

I AM AT A HEIGHT OF 11,400ft on the north-west ridge of
Mount Lester. I am sitting on a boulder, my legs drawn up, my
arms wrapped around them and my chin resting on my knees.
I am spellbound by the view in front of me. A horseshoe of ser-
rated peaks surrounds a deep basin floored by a ribbon of
lakes. Waterfalls tumble from one lake to another, their distant
rumblings primordially soothing. The pinnacled ridges that
link the peaks seem impossibly fragile and unearthly. In the
foreground Island Lake guards the entrance to the basin, delin-
eating it to perfection. A lone tent by the shore gives human
scale to the scene.

It is late in the evening. The last rays of the dying sun cling
to the summits as the shades of night creep ever higher up rock

faces and across snowfields. The only sound is the muted roar of the waterfalls and the rush of the bitter, penetrating wind. I am cold and have no torch to light my descent, but I cannot move. I am stunned into immobility. The panorama before me is almost painfully beautiful. I feel privileged.

I have tried many times to understand my passion for mountains, but whenever it seems that I am beginning to approach some modicum of enlightenment I see a Titcomb Basin and I am once again totally bemused. Perhaps some things will always remain beyond human comprehension.

At length, when the sun quits the summits to redden the clouds, I flee to the valley. Not once do I look back. But I make a promise to myself.

Some other books published by **LUATH** PRESS

Mountain Days & Bothy Nights

Dave Brown and Ian Mitchell

ISBN 0 946487 15 4 PBK £7.50

 Acknowledged as a classic of mountain writing still in demand ten years after its first publication, this book takes you into the bothies, howffs and dosses on the Scottish hills. Fishgut Mac, Desperate Dan and Stumpy the Big Yin stalk hill and public house, evading gamekeepers and Royalty with a camaraderie which was the trademark of Scots hillwalking in the early days.

'The fun element comes through… how innocent the social polemic seems in our nastier world of today… the book for the rucksack this year.'
Hamish Brown, SCOTTISH MOUNTAINEERING CLUB JOURNAL

Scotland's Mountains before the Mountaineers

Ian Mitchell

ISBN 0 946487 39 1 PBK £9.99

 In this ground-breaking book, Ian Mitchell tells the story of explorations and ascents in the Scottish Highlands in the days before mountaineering became a popular sport – when bandits, Jacobites, poachers and illicit distillers traditionally used the mountains as sanctuary. The book also gives a detailed account of the map makers, road builders, geologists, astronomers and naturalists, many of whom ascended hitherto untrodden summits while working in the Scottish Highlands.

Scotland's Mountains before the Mountaineers is divided into four Highland regions, with a map of each region showing key summits. While not designed primarily as a guide, it will be a useful handbook for walkers and climbers. Based on a wealth of new research, this book offers a fresh perspective that will fascinate climbers and mountaineers and everyone interested in the history of mountaineering, cartography, the evolution of landscape and the social history of the Scottish Highlands.

The Highland Geology Trail

John L Roberts

ISBN 0946487 36 7 PBK £5.99

 Where can you find the oldest rocks in Europe?
Where can you see ancient hills around 800 million years old?
How do you tell whether a valley was carved out by a glacier, not a river?
What are the Fucoid Beds?
Where do you find rocks folded like putty?
How did great masses of rock pile up like snow in front of a snow-plough?
When did volcanoes spew lava and ash to form Skye, Mull and Rum?
Where can you find fossils on Skye?

'…a lucid introduction to the geological record in general, a jargon-free exposition of the regional background, and a series of descriptions of specific localities of geological interest on a "trail" around the highlands.
Having checked out the local references on the ground, I can vouch for their accuracy and look forward to investigating farther afield, informed by this guide.
Great care has been taken to explain specific terms as they occur and, in so doing, John Roberts has created a resource of great value which is eminently usable by anyone with an interest in the outdoors…the best bargain you are likely to get as a geology book in the foreseeable future.'
Jim Johnston, PRESS AND JOURNAL

But n Ben A-Go-Go

Matthew Fitt

ISBN 0 946487 82 0 HB £10.99
ISBN 1 84282 041 1 PB £6.99

The year is 2090. Global flooding has left most of Scotland under water. The descendants of those who survived God's Flood live in a community of floating island parishes, known collectively as Port. Port's citizens live in mortal fear of Senga, a supervirus whose victims are kept in a giant hospital

warehouse in sealed capsules called Kists. Paolo Broon is a low-ranking cyberjanny. His life-partner, Nadia, lies forgotten and alone in Omega Kist 624 in the Rigo Imbeki Medical Center. When he receives an unexpected message from his radge criminal father to meet him at But n Ben A-Go-Go, Paolo's life is changed forever. He must traverse VINE, Port and the Drylands and deal with rebel American tourists and crabbit Dundonian microchips to discover the truth about his family's past in order to free Nadia from the sair grip of the merciless Senga. Set in a distinctly unbonnie future-Scotland, the novel's dangerous atmosphere and psychologically-malkied characters weave a tale that both chills and intrigues. In But n Ben A-Go-Go Matthew Fitt takes the allegedly dead language of Scots and energises it with a narrative that crackles and fizzes with life.

an entertaining and ground-breaking book
EDWIN MORGAN

... if you can't get hold of a copy, mug somebody
MARK STEPHEN, SCOTTISH CONNECTION, BBC RADIO SCOTLAND

...the last man who tried anything like this was Hugh MacDiarmid MICHAEL FRY, TODAY PROGRAMME, BBC RADIO 4

Bursting with sly humour, staggeringly imaginative, often poignant and at times exploding with Uzi-blazing action, this book is a cracker...
With Matthew Fitt's book I began to think and sometimes dream in Scots. GREGOR STEELE, TIMES EDUCATIONAL SUPPLEMENT

On the Trail of Queen Victoria in the Highlands

Ian R. Mitchell
UK ISBN 0 946487 79 0 PBK £7.99

How many Munros did Queen Victoria bag?
What 'essential services' did John Brown perform for Victoria?
(and why was Albert always tired?)
How many horses (to the nearest hundred) were needed to undertake a Royal Tour?
What happens when you send a republican

on the tracks of Queen Victoria in the Highlands?
a.. you get a book somewhat more interesting than the usual run of the mill royalist biographies!

Ian R. Mitchell took up the challenge of attempting to write with critical empathy on the peregrinations of Vikki Regina in the Highlands, and about her residence at Balmoral, through which a neo-feudal fairyland was created on Upper Deeside. The expeditions, social rituals and iconography of that world are explored and exploded from within, in what Mitchell terms a Bolshevisation of Balmorality. He follows in Victoria's footsteps throughout the Cairngorms and beyond, to the further reaches of the Highlands. On this journey, a grudging respect and even affection for Vikki ('the best of the bunch') emerges.

The book is designed to enable the armchair/motorised reader, or walker, to follow in the steps of the most widely-travelled royal personage in the Highlands since Bonnie Prince Charlie had wandered there a century earlier.

Index map and 12 detailed maps
21 walks in Victoria's footsteps
Rarely seen Washington Wilson photographs
Colour and black and white reproductions of contemporary paintings
On the Trail of Queen Victoria in the Highlands will also appeal to those with an interest in the social and cultural history of Scotland and the Highlands - and the author, ever-mindful of his own 'royalties', hopes the declining band of monarchists might also be persuaded to give the book a try.

The Supernatural Highlands

Francis Thompson
ISBN 0 946487 31 6 PBK £8.99

An authoritative exploration of the otherworld of the Highlander, happenings and beings hitherto thought to be outwith the ordinary forces of nature. A simple introduction to the way of life of rural Highland and Island communities, this new edition weaves a path through second sight, the evil eye, witchcraft, ghosts, fairies and other supernatural beings, offering new sight-lines on areas of belief once dismissed as folklore and superstition.

Luath Press Limited
committed to publishing well written books worth reading

LUATH PRESS takes its name from Robert Burns, whose little collie Luath (*Gael.*, swift or nimble) tripped up Jean Armour at a wedding and gave him the chance to speak to the woman who was to be his wife and the abiding love of his life. Burns called one of *The Twa Dogs* Luath after Cuchullin's hunting dog in *Ossian's Fingal*. Luath Press was established in 1981 in the heart of Burns country, and is now based a few steps up the road from Burns' first lodgings on Edinburgh's Royal Mile.

Luath offers you distinctive writing with a hint of unexpected pleasures.

Most bookshops in the UK, the US, Canada, Australia, New Zealand and parts of Europe either carry our books in stock or can order them for you. To order direct from us, please send a £sterling cheque, postal order, international money order or your credit card details (number, address of cardholder and expiry date) to us at the address below. Please add post and packing as follows: UK – £1.00 per delivery address; overseas surface mail – £2.50 per delivery address; overseas airmail – £3.50 for the first book to each delivery address, plus £1.00 for each additional book by airmail to the same address. If your order is a gift, we will happily enclose your card or message at no extra charge.

Luath Press Limited
543/2 Castlehill
The Royal Mile
Edinburgh EH1 2ND
Scotland
Telephone: 0131 225 4326 (24 hours)
Fax: 0131 225 4324
email: gavin.macdougall@luath.co.uk
Website: www.luath.co.uk